Decorative Artist's Guide to

Realistic PAINTING

Patti DeRenzo, CDA

NORTH LIGHT BOOKS

CINCINNATI, OHIO
www.artistsnetwork.com

About the Author

Patti DeRenzo, CDA, has been painting for over twenty-four years. After many years of taking instruction from top oil painters while using acrylic paints, Patti has perfected her own unique style of acrylic blending and is the leader in this field. She is an accredited Ann Kingslan teacher, the only one to accomplish this using an acrylic gouache. Patti has authored seven books, thirteen theory booklets, four videos and numerous pattern packets. She now spends much of her time traveling nationally and internationally, teaching for shops and chapters. Patti is the mother of three children—Forest, 24; Travis, 21; and Rebecca, 15. She and her husband, Ken, have been married for over twenty-five years and reside in a small mountain community in southern California.

Library of Congress Cataloging-in-Publication Data

DeRenzo, Patti
   Decorative artist's guide to realistic painting / Patti DeRenzo
      p. cm.
   Includes index.
   ISBN 0-89134-995-2 (pbk.: alk. paper)
   1. Painting—Technique. 2. Realism in art. I. Title.
ND1471 .D47 2001
751.4'26--dc21   2001030990

Editor: Christine Doyle
Production Coordinator: Emily Gross
Designer: Joanna Detz
Layout Artist: Linda Watts
Photographer: Al Parrish

METRIC CONVERSION CHART		
TO CONVERT	TO	MULTIPLY BY
Inches	Centimeters	2.54
Centimeters	Inches	0.4
Feet	Centimeters	30.5
Centimeters	Feet	0.03
Yards	Meters	0.9
Meters	Yards	1.1
Sq. Inches	Sq. Centimeters	6.45
Sq. Centimeters	Sq. Inches	0.16
Sq. Feet	Sq. Meters	0.09
Sq. Meters	Sq. Feet	10.8
Sq. Yards	Sq. Meters	0.8
Sq. Meters	Sq. Yards	1.2
Pounds	Kilograms	0.45
Kilograms	Pounds	2.2
Ounces	Grams	28.4
Grams	Ounces	0.04

This book is dedicated to my Lord and Savior Jesus Christ, whom I gladly thank for my artistic talent. "Each one should use whatever gift he has received to serve others, faithfully administering God's grace in its various forms. If anyone speaks, he should do it as one speaking the very words of God. If anyone serves, he should do it with the strength God provides, so that in all things God may be praised through Jesus Christ. To him be the glory and power for ever and ever. Amen."

1 Peter 4:10-11

Acknowledgments

An undertaking of this magnitude involved the help and prayers of many special people in my life—I can't even imagine what I would have done without them.

My husband and best friend, Ken, for always being there to help me and give me praise even if I was in the middle of a PMS tantrum. You and God, dear, make life possible.

My daughter, Rebecca, for her honest opinions and outstanding sense of color and design.

The New Wine Christian Fellowship women's study for their prayers.

Dawn Fischle, my personal typesetter, for making my scribbles legible and always coming through for me.

Debbie Cole for her prayers and words of encouragement when I was too tired to think straight.

Dee Silver of Silver Brush Limited for superior-quality brushes and patience in developing the DeRenzo Blending Brushes.

Vicki Rhodes and Jim Cobb from Chroma Acrylics for their willingness to always be helpful.

Jim Rosa, Dallas Fischer and Ted Zogg—the wonderful wood men in my life.

Kathy Kipp of North Light Books for approaching me with the idea to do this book.

And especially Christine Doyle, my editor from North Light Books, who was always kind, encouraging and never lost her patience. Thank you for holding my hand through this whole process.

Table of Contents

Introduction
A Focus on Realism

When my son Forest brought home his first painting from kindergarten and told me it was an apple, it was believable because of the round shape and the red color. However, unlike a child's simple painting, the ultimate goal of a still-life artist is to bring to life—on a flat plane or painting surface—the illusion that the painting not only has color harmony and shape recognition, but is three-dimensional, composed of height, depth and width.

I am living proof that artistic ability is not only a God-given gift but also a burning desire to learn the basic elements of art. It is my hope to share with you some skills, techniques and basic art theory so you, too, may experience the joy of expressing yourself through art.

I ask that you start at the beginning of this book, take notes for yourself and expand upon the theory and painting exercises. No one ever became a great chef simply by reading a cookbook. Knowledge comes through experience and making mistakes. Don't be afraid of your mistakes, but learn from them. You need to realize that, with the knowledge and experience you have at this moment, this is the best you can do today. Tomorrow you will be better. Art is a blessing to be appreciated one day at a time.

CHAPTER ONE

Materials

As with any new endeavor, it is important to obtain the proper supplies. These supplies usually can be purchased from your local tole and decorative painting shop or art supply store. If you have problems locating a store in your area, contact the National Society of Decorative Painters, 393 North McLean Boulevard, Wichita, Kansas 67203-5968, (316) 269-9300. They can direct you to the shop nearest you.

General Supplies

Palette Knife
A good-quality palette knife is one with a wooden handle that crooks at the neck and a blade at least 2½ inches (6.4cm) long for mixing colors and values. Both Loew-Cornell and Langnickel produce a good-quality palette knife.

Sponge Roller
A sponge roller is used to paint an eggshell finish on a background. I recommend a roller brush by Padco or you may use a good-quality roller purchased from a home improvement center. Just be sure it produces a very fine texture.

Tracing Paper
First trace all designs onto tracing paper with a pencil so that any adjustments can be easily erased and corrected. A medium-quality tracing paper works well. Purchase either 9" x 12" (23 x 30.5cm) or 11" x 14" (28 x 35.6cm) tracing paper.

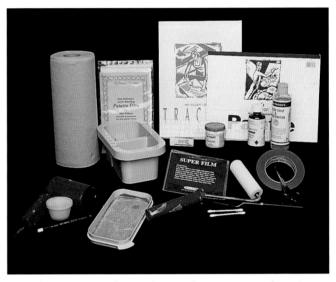

As with any new endeavor, having the proper supplies gives you greater opportunity for success.

Pencil
Trace all designs with a pencil to allow for corrections. Then transfer the pattern to the surface with a pencil so as not to mar or indent the surface. A no. 2 pencil works well for this.

Eraser
I prefer a soft, nonabrasive art eraser. These are sold at art supply or stationery stores.

Painter's Masking Tape
This tape is designed to prevent leakage and has less adhesive, so it won't pull up the background paint when it is removed. It can be purchased from any local hardware or paint store. I recommend Ace or 3M brands.

Transparent Graph Ruler
Use this ruler for keeping still-life designs in alignment vertically and horizontally, and for tracing all straight lines. It can be purchased at most stationery supply stores.

Brush Soap
A good-quality brush soap and conditioner are needed, and they should be designed to remove acrylic paint. I recommend DecoArt or Faux Meister's.

Odorless Solvent
I don't remove graphite lines by erasing them, because, if the paint is still a bit tender, the eraser may damage it. Since the graphite lines are oil-based and I use water-

based paint, odorless solvent removes the graphite lines without harming the paint. I recommend Archival Odorless Solvent or any odorless turpentine.

Wood Filler
Wood filler is used for filling nail holes, wood seams or any background imperfections. I recommend Jo Sonja's Water Based Wood Filler because it dries in a very short time and is easily sanded to a smooth finish.

Cotton Swabs
Any brand of cotton swabs works well for removing unwanted paint or glazing from small areas.

Containers to Hold Mediums
You will need small, open containers to hold the Retarder and Antiquing Medium, Clear Glazing Medium and varnish. I have found that the small disposable cups used in Crystal Light containers work well.

Water Basin
I prefer the brush basin from Loew-Cornell that has the divider in the middle to hold the brushes immersed in water and the ridges on the bottom that you can pull the brush across to remove the paint pigment. This particular basin has a wet palette holder that fits on top as the lid. It usually can be purchased at tole specialty shops or craft centers with tole sections.

Waxed Palette
I prefer to use disposable palette paper that is plastic coated. All of my paints are mixed on a waxed palette before they are transferred onto a wet palette. A disposable oil palette doesn't work because it pulls the moisture out of the paint. A convenient size is 9" x 12" (23 x 30.5cm). It can be purchased at art supply stores or craft and hobby stores.

Sandpaper and Super Film
Several grades of sandpaper—320-, 400- and 600-grit—are used for sanding wood and Masonite inserts to a refined finish. They can be purchased at any hardware store. Super Film, from Houston Art Frame, or 1000-grit sandpaper, is used for sanding between coats of varnish. It usually can be purchased at home decor centers and auto supply stores.

Brown Paper Bag
I use a small piece of paper torn from a brown grocery bag for the final sanding, or buffing, of the background before I start painting.

Paper Towels
I exclusively use blue shop towels by Scott. They are more absorbent than any other paper towel on the market and have the least amount of lint. I also use these in my wet palette setup. They can be purchased at Costco, Sam's Club, Wal-Mart and KMart and are usually found in the auto supply section.

Spritzer Bottle
This can be purchased at a variety store or beauty supply store. Any time I'm going to be away from my painting for a day or two, I lightly mist the top of my paints with water from the spritzer bottle and pour a small amount of water under the paper towel. I then put on an airtight lid.

Hair Dryer
Any good hair dryer works well, but I prefer one that has a cool air button to cool the surface back to room temperature.

Transfer Paper
You will need two different colors of graphite paper: gray for transferring designs onto light-colored backgrounds, and white for transferring designs onto dark-colored backgrounds. Look for graphite that is waxless, greaseless, nonsmearing and smudge-proof. Most art supply stores will sell it in single sheets. Never use carbon paper as it will create a terrible mess and cannot be removed from the painting surface.

Scissors
Any small, sharp scissors work well. I use small embroidery scissors.

Lint-Free Cloth
Never use a tack cloth to remove sanding dust or lint particles. Tack cloths contain oil products that can leave an oil residue on the surface that is not compatible with water-based paints, mediums and varnishes. An old, well-washed flannel shirt or T-shirt works well.

Brushes

Because I use water-based paints and mediums and frequently rinse my brush in water during painting, I strongly recommend using high-quality synthetic brushes.

For any background basecoating that cannot be done with a sponge roller, I use a ¾-inch (19mm) or 1-inch (25mm) **flat or wash brush** (2008S Square Wash) by Silver Brush Ltd. For the actual painting, I use short, flat **chisel blenders** and filberts because of my particular blending style. I blend one value into the next rather than layer one value on top of another. The shorter bristles are specifically designed for blending paint; longer bristle brushes are used for floating or layering. A specialized line of multimedia chisel blenders that lends itself to my particular style of blending is the 5020S Chisel Blender, nos. 2, 4, 6, 8, 10, 12, 14 and 16. For smooth blending, it is best to use the largest brush you can for the specific area.

The 5003S Blending Stroke Filberts nos. 2, 4, 6, 8, 10 and 12 are shorter and rounder than most other **filberts** on the market. They are also designed for blending the paint values together while maintaining proper brush control. The filberts are used mainly when blending round objects such as fruit, flowers and eggs.

After I have blended and created the form of the object being painted, I enhance the painting by adding highlights, shines, shadows and reflected light with layered glazing using **angle brushes**. For this, I recommend the 5006S Blending Floating Angular brushes. Because they are angled and come to a sharp point, they are easier to control in the tiny triangular areas where shadows begin. They can be flattened out into larger shaded areas.

Mops are used to soften the glazing and layering stages so that no harsh lines appear. I use the ⅛-inch (3mm), ¼-inch (6mm) and ⅜-inch (10mm) 5319S Wee Mops, and the 5019S Refining Mop no. 8 for these techniques. For antiquing and softening blended backgrounds, I use the 5518S White Round Mop nos. 14 through 20. The 3-inch (76mm) 9092S Studio Blending Softener works very well for extra-large backgrounds.

The 1721S Stencil Mini **dry brushes** are used in the enhancement stage for adding the first layers of highlighting. Use the appropriate size for the area needed. They come in sizes 0, 2, 4 and 6.

The 2407S Ultra Mini Script **liner** no. 20/0 is used for fine lines and writing. The 2400S Ultra Mini Pointed Round no. 12/0 is used for pulling small design strokes. Other liners I use include the 2522S Monogram Liner nos. 0 and 1 for blending areas like the rims and handles of cups, and the 2500S Round no. 000.

For varnishing, I use a 1-inch (25mm) 2514S Wash, which produces a smooth finish showing no brushstrokes.

Chisel Blenders
The 5020S Chisel Blender is available in sizes 2 through 16.

Filberts
The 5003S Blending Stroke Filbert is available in sizes 2 through 12.

Angle Brushes
The 5006S Blending Floating Angular brush comes in sizes ⅛-inch (3mm), ¼-inch (6mm), ½-inch (12mm) and ¾-inch (19mm).

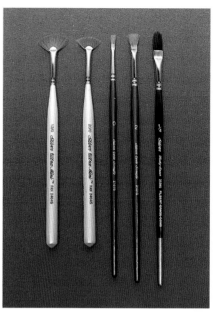

Large Mop Brushes
The 5518S Mop comes in sizes 14, 16 and 20. The 3-inch (76mm) 9092S Studio Blending Softener is used for softening extra large areas or cabinets.

Small Mop Brushes
The 5319S Wee Mop comes in sizes ⅛-inch (3mm), ¼-inch (6mm) and ⅜-inch (10mm). I recommend using the 5019S Refining Mop no. 8 as well.

Specialty Brushes
The 2404S Ultra Mini Fan comes in sizes 12/0 and 20/0. The 2101S Cole Scruffy brush is available in nos. 0 and 2. I also use the ¼-inch (6mm) 2528S Filbert Grass Comb.

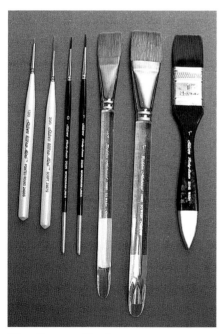

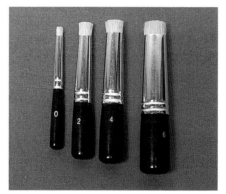

Stencil Brushes
The 1721S Stencil Mini brush is available in sizes 0, 2, 4 and 6.

Miscellaneous Brushes
The liners I use are the 2407S Ultra Mini Script no. 20/0, 2522S Monogram nos. 0 and 1, and 2400S Ultra Mini no. 12/0. The ¾-inch (19mm) and 1-inch (25mm) 2008S Square Wash are used for blending large backgrounds, applying Retarder and Antiquing Medium and basecoating backgrounds. For varnishing, I use the 1-inch (25mm) 2514S Wash.

 ## *Cleaning Brushes*

Remember: Even though Jo Sonja's paints are an acrylic gouache, they are still in an acrylic carrier. The paints are very brush friendly and don't dry in the ferrule as some other acrylics can. When you are finished painting for the day, saturate the brushes in retarder, let them sit for a few minutes and then loosen any paint with your fingers. Wash well with Faux Meister's brush soap and water, rinse and air dry.

Paints

I use Jo Sonja's Chroma Acrylic paints and mediums exclusively. Jo Sonja's paints are unlike any other acrylic in the decorative painting market. They are blendable, much like oils, with the quick drying time of an acrylic paint. They provide you with quality lightfast pigments and long-term durability, and they clean up with soap and water.

Jo Sonja's is not just another acrylic paint—it is an acrylic gouache. So what does this actually mean? A true gouache is a highly pigmented opaque watercolor that can be reactivated indefinitely with water. In fact, you need to put a sealer over the finished artwork to protect it from water. Jo Sonja's paint is a gouache in a polymer acrylic carrier. This means that the paint cures 80% in twenty-four hours and 100% in two to three weeks, depending upon the humidity in your area. This allows the paint to be reactivated.

Because you have the ability to blend one value into another, rather than only layer values like you do with bottled acrylics, you are able to achieve an added depth of realism. It's a paint in a class of its own—a bridge between oil and acrylic.

Jo Sonja's paints are an acrylic polymer gouache that is a pure pigment paint—rich in color, with blendability, which allows for realism and depth. There are a total of seventy pure palette colors, five iridescents and five metallics.

Mediums

All Purpose Sealer

All Purpose Sealer allows one-step basecoating when it is mixed with Jo Sonja's paints. The mix seals and basecoats the surface in one easy step and provides "tooth" to the surface for proper adhesion. I mix two parts paint with one part All Purpose Sealer (2:1). Apply two coats to any given wood surface, drying and sanding between coats.

For sealing clear wood, mix seven parts All Purpose Sealer with one part water (7:1). Apply it with a soft brush. When you are done, make sure to thoroughly wash the brush with soap and water. Sealing clear wood in this manner raises the grain slightly, so simply sand with 400-grit sandpaper and remove any sanding dust with a slightly moist lint-free cloth.

Flow Medium

Flow Medium is used to thin down paints and mediums instead of using water, which dilutes the strength of the paint. When a small amount of Flow Medium is added to the paint or background color, it produces thinner, smoother paint layers and a more refined surface.

Retarder and Antiquing Medium

Retarder and Antiquing Medium is used in several different techniques and applications. It is considered the "medium" for Jo Sonja's paints, as opposed to water, which is traditionally used with acrylic paints. Instead of dipping the brush into water, dip it into the Retarder and Antiquing Medium. Think of water as an eraser only. Water is used only to clean up any unwanted paint on the background or to quickly clean the paint pigment out of the brush.

Retarder and Antiquing Medium is also applied to a painted surface that has been basecoated in values for wet-on-wet blending and refining. It is used any time you want transparency, such as when painting glass and water drops. It is also used for all of my glazing techniques, accents, turning colors, highlights, shading, shadows, reflected colors, reflected lights, rouging and antiquing.

Clear Glazing Medium

I refer to the Clear Glazing Medium as an isolator or barrier coat. It is a sealer with porosity, which means it can be used to lightly seal the painted surface but is porous enough for the paint to adhere to for the glazing and color enhancement stage. Once the Clear Glazing Medium has been applied to the surface, you can no longer reactivate the paint with retarder.

When the Clear Glazing Medium dries, it allows you to continue with semitransparent and transparent layering techniques. It builds up enough space between paint layers so that light can enter into the painting, just like it does with egg tempera painting or the oil glazing of the Old Masters. Also, by sealing off the painting surface you are content with, you make your painting mistake-proof. If you make a mistake with the highlights, shading, reflected light or reflected color, you can simply remove it with a soft rag or cotton swab and a little water. Do not apply more than three coats of Clear Glazing Medium in a twenty-four-hour period. If it becomes tacky, allow it to dry ten to twelve hours before continuing.

Be sure to wash your brush immediately afterward with soap and water.

Wood Stain Gels
These unique water-based stains are transparent pigments in a Clear Glazing Medium base. This produces a glowing transparent stain without the "milking" or "hazing" associated with other acrylics. The wood stains may be mixed with other paints and mediums in Jo Sonja's line.

Stroke and Blending Medium
The Stroke and Blending Medium is thicker than the Retarder and Antiquing Medium. Because of its heavier consistency, a small puddle placed on my waxed palette

will remain moist all day. Any time my paint has dried and I want to lightly blend a bit more, I dress the brush in the Stroke and Blending Medium and gently apply it to the desired area. Stroke and Blending Medium can be thinned with Retarder and Antiquing Medium.

Background Colors
Jo Sonja's Background colors have a flattening agent added to them, which makes them ideal for basecoating backgrounds. I generally use two parts background color plus one part All Purpose Sealer (2:1). The background colors can be intermixed or Jo Sonja's tube colors may be added to achieve the color of choice.

Polyurethane Water Based Varnishes
All of my paintings are done using Jo Sonja's Chroma Acrylics and then varnished with the Polyurethane Water Based Varnishes. Personally, I found that the matte varnish has too much matting agent and the gloss varnish is too shiny or glossy, so I mix the two. You can vary the levels of sheen in the gloss varnish with the amount of matte varnish you mix in. Experiment until you find the formula that suits your personal preference. My favorite is one part matte varnish to one part gloss varnish (1:1).

Jo Sonja's Background Colors come in twenty-six different colors. There are ten different water-based wood stain gels.

Jo Sonja's mediums are specially formulated to be compatible and intermixable with the complete Jo Sonja line.

Paint Saver Palette and Palette Film

I can't stress enough the importance of keeping the paint at a creamy consistency. During the past few years, I've had calls from students across the country who were struggling with this problem. Either their paints had dried out and become gooey, or they had become so wet that they ran together into a soupy mess. I suggest using a wet palette setup, which seems to alleviate a lot of the problems.

Wet Palette Setup

I use the Paint Saver Palette by Loew-Cornell. It's airtight and the perfect size for my needs with a depth of one inch. To set it up, fold two shop towels in half (this will make four thicknesses of shop towels) and cut them to fit the bottom of the recessed plastic dish.

Thoroughly wet the shop towel and gently squeeze out the excess water, but leave enough so that it will still be quite wet. Stretch the shop towel to remove any wrinkles and place it on the bottom of the plastic dish. Smooth out any wrinkles or air pockets, pushing them out with your fingers. Next, cut a piece of palette film ¼-inch (0.6cm) smaller than the shop towel. Then gently place the dry film on top of the wet shop towel. Press the two together so they form a bond, and push out any air bubbles. If the film does not adhere to the towel, the shop towel is probably not wet enough.

After a few hours of painting, you might notice the palette film starting to dry and pull away from the shop towel. When this starts to happen, pour a small amount of water—and I emphasize, *small*—under the shop towel. You will be able to see the film soak up the water. You might need to poke down the outer edges of the film so that it again bonds to the shop towel. If you pour in too much water, the paints will become too runny.

If the paint starts to form a dried film on top, pour a little water under the towel, put the lid on top and take a fifteen-minute break. I make it a habit to put the lid back on the wet palette every time I leave my painting table. If I won't be painting for a week or so, not only will I pour water under the shop towel, but I will also mist the top of the paints with water from my spritzer bottle.

When traveling in a car, place the wet palette on the floorboard and remove the lid. There is something about the warmth and motion of the car that causes the paints to run together when you have the lid on. Remember, it is *extremely important* to keep these paints wet and at a creamy consistency.

After a few weeks, you might notice that your paints are smelling musty and moldy. To alleviate this problem, use distilled water or add a few drops of bleach to the water. Bobbie Takashima recommends using copper pennies at the corners inside the wet palette to help solve this problem because copper retards mold growth.

Tip

Many students have contacted me about their difficulty in finding a place where they can purchase nonwax palette film. You can now purchase this product directly from me at my seminars or by mail. See the resources on page 127.

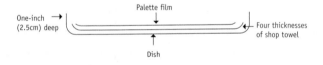

One-inch (2.5cm) deep

Palette film

Four thicknesses of shop towel

Dish

For your wet palette, use a small dish no more than one-inch (2.5cm) deep with a lid (Loew-Cornell's Paint Saver Palette is an excellent choice), shop towels and palette film.

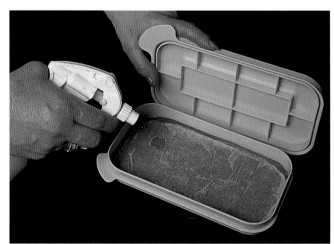

To reactivate gooey paint, pour water under the paper towel, mist with a spray bottle and cover the palette with a lid for fifteen minutes.

CHAPTER TWO

Elements of Art

It's difficult to fully understand art until you understand the primary elements. The basic elements of realistic still-life painting are color, value, intensity, temperature and form.

Value

Value, or tone as it is sometimes referred to, is the degree of lightness or darkness of a color. Value is the most important aspect of a painting because value creates form, dimension and realism.

To better understand value we will refer to a gray value scale, which is used to define shades of gray plus white and black.

When color is incorporated into the value scale system, it is like being Dorothy and going from black-and-white Kansas to the colorful Land of Oz. Each color has a value of its own. Yellow is the lightest value color and violet is the darkest value color.

By learning to control the value of the colors in your painting you can determine where you want the viewer to look first. Strong, or wide, value contrast within and between objects can be used to separate or divide objects. Close values unite objects and demand less attention and can become a bridge from one object to the next to create harmony. Having control of value lets you set up a center of interest in your painting, which is where the greatest amount of value change will occur.

All of my paintings are done with a value scale of color, using anywhere from three to seven values for each element.

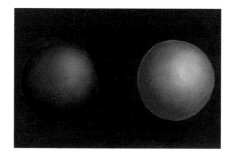

At left, the two light spheres are painted with the same values, as are the two dark spheres. Any time there is a high contrast between a painted object and the background (such as the dark sphere on the light background), it gives the appearance that the object is coming forward.

Black	Low Dark	Dark	High Dark	Medium	Low Light	Light	Highlight	White

Low Dark	Dark	High Dark	Medium	Low Light	Light	Highlight

Violet	Blue-Violet	Red-Violet	Blue	Blue-Green	Green	Red-Orange	Red	Orange	Yellow-Orange	Yellow-Green	Yellow	

The gray value scale is shown above. The colored scale is neither lighter nor darker than the gray scale—they are of equal value.

Intensity

Intensity is the brightness or dullness of a color. The root word "intense" means extreme, powerful or highly concentrated. A color is most intense in its pure pigment form. Any time you add one color to another you change or lower its intensity. Intense or bright should not be confused with light and dark. A color can be very dark and still be very bright or intense, as it is with a pure violet.

Intensity of color can be used to establish the center of interest in a painting. The most intense colors are used in small amounts in the center of interest, with the intensity of the surrounding objects gradually decreasing. The least intense colors are used for the background. The gradation from high intensity to low intensity gives the illusion of depth within a painting.

So how does one control or lower the intensity of a color? There are several possibilities to choose from. With a little experience, you'll be able to determine which of the following will work in any given situation.

Ways to Adjust Intensity

Adding Background Color
One of my favorite ways to dull colors is to add my chosen background color to all color mixes. This helps to establish color harmony throughout the entire painting. Some artists refer to this as using a "mother color."

Adding White
When white is added to a color, it not only lowers the intensity and weakens the pure color, but it raises and lightens the value.

Adding Black
Black added to a color lowers the intensity and the value. It is also a method of shading a color.

Adding Gray
Gray also neutralizes intense colors. Since we know that white raises a color's value and black lowers a color's value, what does gray do to the values? That depends upon the value of gray being added to the color. If I have a light value color that I want to neutralize but not change the value, for example, yellow-orange, then I would add a light value gray (refer to the gray value scale). If I wanted to tone a dark value color like blue, I would use a high dark value gray. Using values of gray is a good way to lower the intensity without changing the value of a color.

Adding a Color's Neighbor
Adding a color's neighbor on the color wheel is another way of neutralizing a color. What is a color's neighbor? It is any color that is right next to (above or below) a color on the color wheel (see the color wheel at right).

The apple on the left was painted with only white and black added to change the intensity and value of the red. The apple on the right appears much more alive because red's neighbors from the color wheel were used to alter its intensity and value.

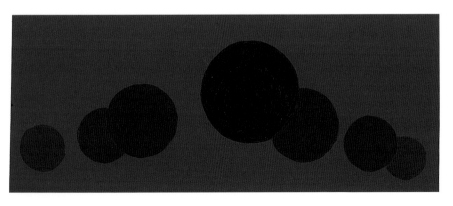

All of the circles and background are painted blue but in graduating degrees of intensity. By shutting your eyes and quickly opening them, you will notice that you see the most intense blue circle (the center one) first. Intensity helps to create a center of interest.

When using a color's neighbor, the color is not dulled and the brightness is not altered. However, the color is no longer pure.

Adding a Color's Complement

A color's complement is the color directly opposite that color on the color wheel. Whenever you add a color's complement, the intensity is lowered, but the value can either be raised or lowered depending on the complementary color's value. For example, when lowering red's intensity with its complementary green, the intensity is lowered but the value (lightness or darkness of the color) remains the same because pure red and pure green are both medium value colors.

Adding an Earth Color

Another way of lowering a color's intensity is to use an earth color. Earth colors are pigments made with chemicals from the earth. Every earth color has a color family in which it belongs. Some earth colors may shift color families depending on the brand of acrylic or oil paint you use. In the chart on pages 124-126, I have listed the earth colors in each color family for Jo Sonja's Chroma Acrylic paints.

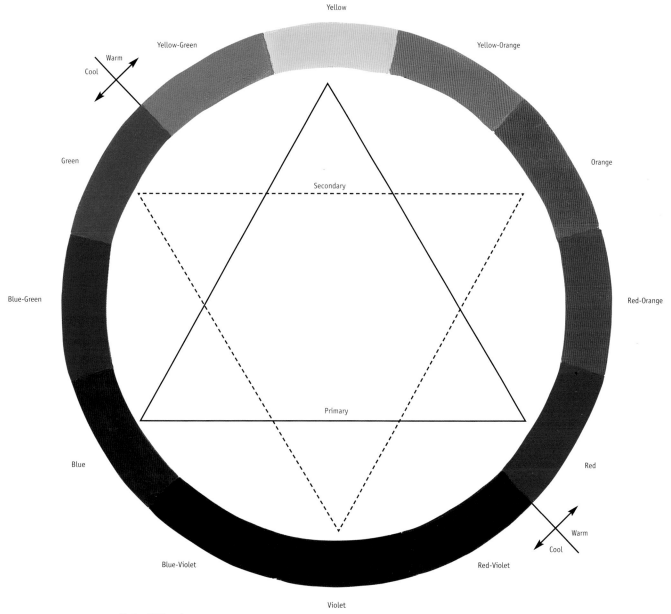

Color Wheel
A color's neighbor is any color that is right next to (above or below) a color on the wheel. Complementary colors are opposite each other on the color wheel.

Using a Toner Color

With Jo Sonja's acrylic paints, I also have the option of lowering a color's intensity with the use of toner color. These colors already have a significant grayness or neutralizing factor in them. Jo Sonja's line has a variety of toner colors from which to choose. Refer to the chart on pages 124-126 for Jo Sonja's toner colors for each color family.

Adding Pure Color

You have been given a lot of options in lowering the intensity of a color or dulling it, but what happens if a color becomes too dull, muddy or chalky? The addition of the pure color back into the mix will clear or brighten the color.

Knowing the color families of the paints you use makes it much easier to use color and intensity. On page 124 I have grouped all Jo Sonja's colors into color families and have included their values and intensities.

Temperature

Temperature, another of our basic elements, also affects the position of an object in a painting because warm colors advance and cool colors recede. However, the temperature of a color is relative to the temperature of the other colors it is next to. It is true that if a warm color is placed on a cool background, the warm color will come forward. And if you place a cool object on a warm background, the cool object comes forward. Just as close values unite and wide values separate, close temperatures unite and opposite temperatures separate. The closer the temperature relationship between an object and the background, the more the object will recede or lose its importance. The stronger the temperature contrast between the background and the object, the more the object will come forward and add depth.

What are considered the warm and cool colors? If you divide the color wheel in half, with a line to the left of yellow-green and to the right of red-violet, all the colors on the right side are the warm colors (see the color wheel on page 15). The colors on the left side are the cool colors. I remember the temperature of colors by associating warm colors with fire and sun (yellow, orange and red) and cool colors with water and sky (blue, green and violet).

Now let's take this one step further. Every color has a warm and cool side; for example, red is considered a warm color. But compare Napthol Red Light to Napthol Crimson. In comparison, Napthol Red Light is warmer and Napthol Crimson is cooler. I find it helpful to know the warm and cool colors in each color family since everyone sees color differently. The temperatures of Jo Sonja's Chroma Acrylics are noted in the chart on page 124.

In these two illustrations, the pink flowers are identical and the blue flowers are identical. On the warm pink background, the cool blue flower comes forward, but on the cool blue background, the blue flower recedes.

Colors have a warm and cool side as illustrated in these primary colors. The cool colors at top are Cadmium Yellow Light, Napthol Crimson and Prussian Blue Hue. The warm colors are Cadmium Yellow Mid, Napthol Red Light and Ultra Blue Deep.

Form

Form is the last element of art we will cover in this chapter. In the world around us, all objects have structure or form. The four basic forms are the sphere, cylinder, cube and cone. Everything we see is made up of one or a combination of these four forms. When these forms are painted in values, they become dimensional, having height, width and depth.

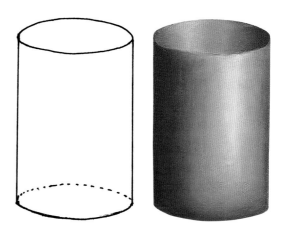

Cylinder

A cylinder is a round shape having two parallel sides. When drawn on paper, the cylinder's depth is usually conveyed with an ellipse drawn at the top. But when painted, values indicate the cylinder as either having a flat top or being open. Some examples of a cylinder are a coffee mug, pencil and crock. Cylinders are frequently used to connect shapes. For example, a sphere connected to a cylinder can be used to paint a lightbulb or the glass shade of a hurricane lamp.

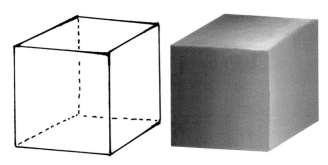

Sphere

When drawn on paper, a sphere is nothing more than a circle or flat disk. But when you think of it as a sphere, it occupies a given space and has dimension. Some obvious examples of a perfect sphere are a baseball, basketball, bubble and orange. Other objects that are modified spheres are an egg, football, nut and apple. Then there are objects that are partial spheres, such as a teacup or bowl.

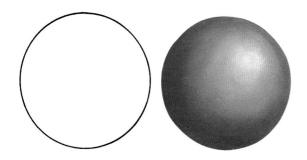

Cube

The cube is a form having six sides: a top, bottom and four walls. When painted as a block, only three sides are visible to the viewer: the top and two sides. When painted as an open box or basket, the viewer sees all four sides. The vertical lines of a cube are always vertical to the horizontal plane. Some examples of cubes are boxes, tabletops, books, doors and baskets.

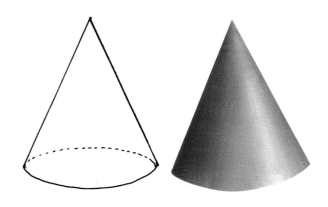

Cone

The cone is probably the least used of all the shapes. Cones are triangular shapes with rounded sides. When drawn on paper, the cone is a triangle with a circle or half ellipse for the third side. The first shape that usually comes to mind is an ice cream cone. Other examples are funnels, carrots, champagne glasses, lamp shades and some seashells.

Take a minute to observe the room around you. How many forms or combination of forms can you identify?

CHAPTER THREE

Background Preparation

Whether you are painting on wood or a Masonite insert, having the proper background preparation is essential to ensuring a smooth, refined painting surface and the overall professionalism of a finished painted piece.

Fill any nail holes or imperfections with wood filler. I prefer Jo Sonja's Water Based Wood Filler because it dries in less than an hour, is easily sanded to a smooth finish and cleans up with soap and water. However, any good-quality brand of wood filler works well. When the wood filler is completely dry, sand the entire surface in the direction of the wood grain to a smooth finish using 400- to 600-grit sandpaper. Remove any dust with a lint-free cloth.

Eggshell Finish

My blending technique requires a surface that is slightly porous—like an eggshell—for the paint to adhere to. You want the finished background surface to feel like refined porcelain with a light matte finish.

To accomplish this, thoroughly wet your sponge roller in water. Squeeze out as much of the water as possible, then blot well on a dry paper towel. At this point, your sponge should hardly feel wet at all.

Place a generous amount of the background color mixed with All Purpose Sealer (2:1) onto your waxed palette. (You may also use Jo Sonja's premixed background colors and All Purpose Sealer mixed two to one.) Roll the sponge roller into the mixed color, then roll it back and forth on the waxed palette until the sponge roller is completely covered with paint.

Tip

Always save some of your mixed background color for touch-up.

Now roll the sponge back and forth on your piece, using a good amount of pressure until the entire surface is covered, reloading the sponge roller only when necessary. (*Note:* Do not apply too much paint to the project. Using less paint will give you a smoother finish.) Keep rolling back and forth. As the paint starts to dry, ease up on your pressure and continue rolling back and forth. Gradually apply less pressure so that the final roll is ever so light. You should see the texture of the paint become finer and more refined.

Wash out the sponge roller, remove any excess moisture, blot the sponge well on a paper towel and let the

Apply wood filler with a palette knife. When dry, sand the surface smooth.

Remove any sanding dust with a slightly dampened, lint-free cloth. Do not use a tack cloth as this will leave an oily residue on the surface.

Moisten the sponge roller in water and remove excess moisture with a paper towel.

Roll the sponge back and forth on the waxed palette, thoroughly covering the sponge with paint.

Roll the sponge on the surface. Putting a piece of plastic or waxed paper under the painting surface makes for easier cleanup. The "eggshell" finish should feel like refined porcelain, not like sandpaper.

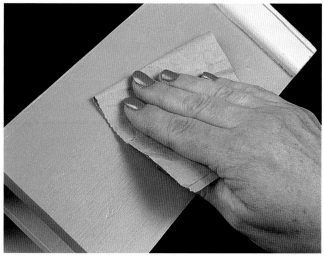

Buff the surface with a piece of brown paper bag to ensure a refined finish.

painted surface dry to the touch. Then sand using 600-grit wet and dry sandpaper. Remove any sanding dust with a lint-free cloth. Apply another coat of paint with your sponge roller using the same technique. Thoroughly dry the surface, and lightly sand or buff with a piece of brown paper bag.

It is important that your surface feels like the outside of an eggshell—slightly porous with just enough tooth for the paint to grab onto, somewhat like porcelain. It

should not feel bumpy like sandpaper or too smooth and slick.

This method of rolling on the background allows you to basecoat and seal the surface at the same time. It provides a solid one-color background, and once this is achieved, you can choose various background applications to paint over the solid color. Following are instructions for creating two-toned, glazed and blended backgrounds.

Two-Toned Background

Once the solid eggshell application is dry, sanded and dusted, place a piece of painter's masking tape across the top edge of the table line or horizon line. Seal down the tape edge with a fingernail or hard piece of plastic (a credit card works well).

Mix the second color with All Purpose Sealer (2:1) and apply it to the surface with a clean, slightly damp sponge roller. Apply this second color in exactly the same way as the solid eggshell finish. Dry, sand and, if needed, apply a second coat. For smaller projects, the second color may be brushed on over the eggshell finish. Be sure to have solid coverage. When dry, remove the painter's tape. In this book, project one on page 34 has a two-toned background.

Painter's tape works well for masking off an area when a second color is to be added. For a small surface, the second color can be brushed on with a ¾-inch (19mm) square wash brush.

Blended Background

A blended background is applied over a solid-covered eggshell finish. It is made up of several different values blended into one another.

When your background is dry, transfer the background placement map—showing where to place the different values of the background color—to the surface. Then apply a generous amount of Retarder and Antiquing Medium with a 1-inch (25mm) wash brush. Blot the brush onto a paper towel, then fully load the brush with the highlight value mix and apply to the surface. Side load the brush into the light value mix and start blending it out toward the outer edge. Keep working the values side by side, blending next into the medium mix, then dark and finally low dark. If the paint starts to dry and tack up, tap your brush into the Retarder and Antiquing Medium to help loosen the paint, and continue to blend. Refine the blend using your no. 20 mop brush. You should have a smooth gradation of values from the lightest to the darkest mix.

Let the paint dry thoroughly. You can speed up the drying time by using a hair dryer, but be sure the surface is back to room temperature before you proceed any further. Because of the use of Retarder and Antiquing Medium, the background will take considerably longer to dry than a solid background. When your surface is dry, brush on one good coat of Clear Glazing Medium to protect it. Project five on page 90 has a blended background.

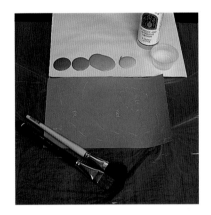

For a blended background, first moisten the surface with Retarder and Antiquing Medium. Have all the values you'll be using on the palette before you begin so you can work quickly.

Blend background values into one another by referring to the background placement map. Start with the lightest values and work toward the darkest.

Use the no. 20 mop brush to further blend and soften, achieving a nice gradation of color.

Glazed Background

A glazed background is also applied over a solid-covered eggshell finish. A glaze is a semitransparent to transparent layer of paint applied to the background, enabling the background color to glow through. This is accomplished by first moistening the entire background surface with Retarder and Antiquing Medium. Moisten a ¾-inch (19mm) angle brush with Retarder and Antiquing Medium, then load the high point of the angle with the glaze color. Blend out the glazing color onto the waxed palette until it is semitransparent. Starting at one edge of the background surface, apply the semitransparent color on top of the Retarder and Antiquing Medium, blending it out until you have a smooth gradation from semitransparent color to transparent color. Finish by softening with a mop brush ranging in size from 1-inch (25mm) to no. 20. The glaze might need to be reapplied several times; allow time for it to dry between layers. When glazes are applied over a background that has been blended, the background takes on an added depth that cannot be achieved in any other way. When dry, brush on one coat of Clear Glazing Medium. Project three on page 62 has a glazed background.

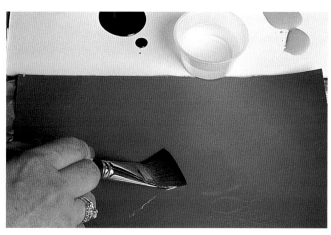

For a glazed background, first apply retarder to the background. A 1-inch (25mm) wash brush works well for this.

Blend the glazing color on a waxed palette until it becomes semitransparent.

Apply the semitransparent paint over the painted surface. Work the color out until it is transparent.

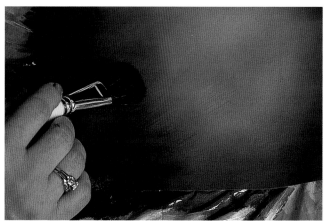

Even out any hard edges with a no. 20 mop brush.

CHAPTER FOUR

Value Blending and Refining

In this chapter, I will cover the basic elements of blending, which include mixing a gray value scale, using a value placement map, holding the brush, positioning the brush properly for blending, blending and basecoating values, and wet-on-wet blending and refining.

Mixing a Gray Value Scale

We have learned that value creates form. And relatively speaking, warm, intense and light colors advance, while cool, dull and dark colors recede. Let's put this knowledge into practice by mixing a simple gray value scale.

Place pure tube colors of Titanium White, Carbon Black and Raw Sienna at the top of your waxed palette. On the next row down, in the center, mix a medium value gray from the white and black. Remember to wipe the palette knife between colors to avoid contaminating the pure colors.

Split the medium value gray into thirds. Move one-third to the right to establish the darker values and one-third to the left to establish the lighter values. Add Carbon Black to the puddle on the right until it is one value darker than the medium value. To the puddle on the left, add Titanium White until it is one value lighter than your medium value.

To the light value, add a very tiny amount of Raw Sienna. This will slight-

Making a Value Scale

When mixing a value scale with any colors, remember these four points:

1. The color listed first is the main body of paint. The colors listed next are to be added in smaller amounts, much like an ingredient label.

2. Wipe the palette knife before picking up additional colors. This will keep you from contaminating your other colors.

3. To make light values darker, add dark values a little at a time to the light values.

4. To make dark values lighter, add light values a little at a time to dark values.

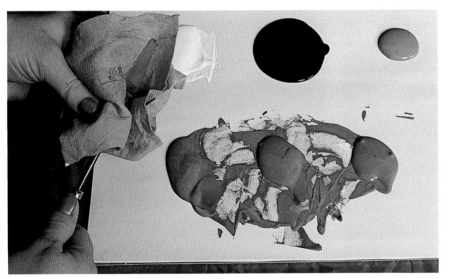

Place the pure colors at the top of the waxed palette and make a medium value gray from white and black. Remember to wipe your palette knife before picking up a new color. Divide the resulting puddle into three equal parts.

ly warm the light value. The white makes the value lighter and brighter, and the Raw Sienna makes it warmer. I chose Raw Sienna because it is a pure color in the yellow family that is neutral enough not to turn the gray color family into green (yellow + black = green). The black naturally makes the dark value darker, duller and cooler.

You have now mixed three values: light, medium and dark.

Split the pile of dark value paint in half. Add more Carbon Black to the pile on the far right, thus establishing a low dark value mix. To mix your fifth value, the highlight value, split your light value in half. To the pile on the far left, add Titanium White until it is one value lighter, and again add the smallest amount of Raw Sienna, just enough to warm the highlight value. If the value takes on a yellow hue, you've added too much Raw Sienna. Try again.

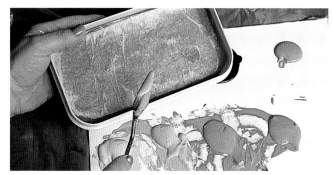

Once the paints have been mixed on a waxed palette, transfer them to a wet palette so they will remain wet, smooth and creamy.

Transfer the mixed values in order from the lightest to the darkest onto a wet palette (see page 12 for wet palette setup). A little later in this chapter, we'll learn to blend values with these colors.

Using a Value Placement Map

A value placement map shows where each value is placed on an object to give that object form and dimension. For each project in this book, I've included a value placement map and a value scale of colors that correspond to each other. On the maps, notice that the values follow the form of the object. The value areas on a sphere are rounded, while the value areas for a cube are linear.

In charting out the values of an object, first establish your light source. I use an upper right-hand light source. This means that my light source is in front of the object, up a bit and to the right, coming from approximately a 45° angle. Then divide your object (for example, a sphere) in half horizontally and then vertically. The high-

light will be in the center of the upper right quadrant, with the low dark being in the crescent of the lower left quadrant because it is farthest from the light source. The rest of the values will follow the form or shape as in the diagram. The medium value covers the largest area of the object, thus it is referred to as the body color.

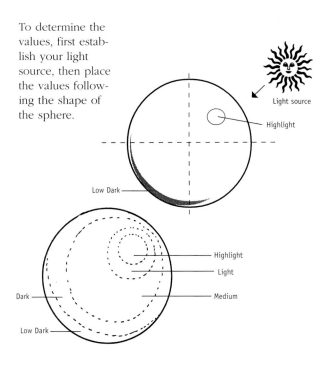

To determine the values, first establish your light source, then place the values following the shape of the sphere.

Light source

Highlight

Low Dark

Highlight

Light

Dark

Medium

Low Dark

For each of the projects in this book, the areas on the value placement map correspond with the values of mixed paint.

More Value Maps

Closed Cylinder

DK — MED
LT
HI LT
DK — MED
DK
LO DK
MED
DK
MED
HI LT
MED
LT

Cone

LO DK — DK
DK — MED
LT
MED
HI LT
LT

Open Cube

MED — DK — LO DK
MED
LT
DK
LO DK — DK — MED — LT
MED
HI LT

The values on the maps have been abbreviated as follows:

Hi Lt = Highlight
Lt = Light
Lo Lt = Low Light
Med = Medium
Hi Dk = High Dark
Dk = Dark
Lo Dk = Low Dark

No matter what the shape of the object, the values always follow that form. The light source for all of these is coming from the right at an approximately 45° angle.

Holding the Brush

This will take some practice, but it is very important to make the brush do the blending for you. Place the brush in the valley between your thumb and index finger so that the brush handle is approximately 3 to 4 inches (7.6 to 10.2cm) up from the metal ferrule. Now place your index finger on top of the brush, pointing to the bristles of the brush. Grip the brush loosely.

Holding the brush in this position, place the bristles at a 33° angle to the painting surface. How can you tell if the brush is at a 33° angle? If you are bending the bristles of the brush, your angle is too high and you are in danger of digging holes in the paint. If you are scraping the metal ferrule against the painting surface, then your angle is too low.

When the brush is held properly, all of the bristles will be in full contact with the painting surface. In this position, you will be able to take full advantage of all the bristles in the brush, ensuring proper blending on your painting surface.

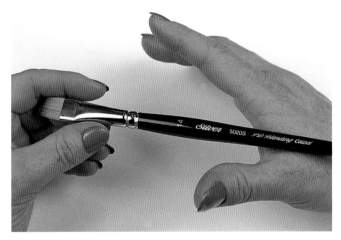

Place the brush in the valley of your thumb and index finger, holding it 3 to 4 inches (7.6 to 10.2cm) from the metal ferrule.

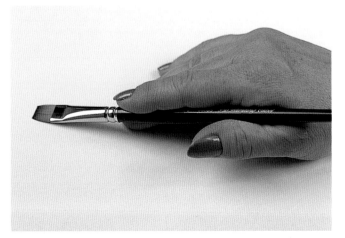

Lightly grasp the brush with your index finger pointing toward the bristles of the brush. Then place the brush at a 33° angle to the painting surface. Only at this angle are you using the brush to its full blending ability.

Blending

For this beginning blending exercise, you will use only the light, medium and dark values you have just mixed.

In the first stage of blending, you need to basecoat the object in values, making sure you have solid coverage and no background showing through. There will be some value change, giving form and dimension to the painted object. Don't worry about perfecting the blending—that will be done in the next step.

To keep this exercise simple, place tape around the outside perimeter of a rectangle that is 3 inches (7.6cm) wide by 1¼ inches (3.2cm) tall. This way full attention can be given to the blending. Divide the rectangle into thirds and label the left-hand third "light," the center third "medium" and the right-hand third "dark."

Dip a no. 10 chisel blender brush into Retarder and Antiquing Medium, blot it on a paper towel and load the brush into the lightest value first—in this case, the light value. Gently tap the loaded brush onto the waxed palette. Hold the brush at a 33° angle to the painting surface, and fill in the light value area.

Once you have filled in the light value area, side load the brush into the next darker value—in this case, the medium value. *Note: Do not* wipe the brush, put it in water or add any retarder.

Gently tap the loaded brush onto your waxed palette to join the two values together. Do not blend the paints on the waxed palette; the actual blending is done on the painting surface.

Hold the brush with the medium value on the right side. Place the brush on the surface with the light half of the brush on the light value area, and the other half on the medium value area. Holding the brush at a 33° angle, start blending the two values together, patting and pulling simultaneously. The brush must pass back and forth between the two values in order to blend the values together and create a middle value in between. Walk the brush to the right, then to the left, then back to the right.

Now with longer strokes, soften the area where the two values meet. Then continue to walk the brush to the right into the medium value area.

Fully load the brush into the medium value paint, tap gently onto the waxed palette and basecoat the rest of the medium value area, filling it in to the line where the medium value and dark value areas meet. Again, side load the brush into the dark value paint, and tap gently on the waxed palette. Place half of the brush on the medium value area, the other half on the dark value area.

Blend the values, walking the brush to the right onto the dark value area. Then walk it back to the left onto the medium value area, then back to the right. Now pull some longer strokes, pulling the paint and blending at the line where the two values come together.

Since Retarder and Antiquing Medium, not water, is the "medium" used, dip the brush first into the retarder.

Blot out the excess retarder onto a paper towel.

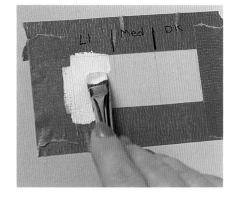

Holding the brush at a 33° angle to the painting surface, fill in the light area. By taping off the rectangle, you can forget about trying to be neat and give your full attention to blending.

Tap the brush onto the waxed palette to remove any excess paint and push the two values together. Do not blend out the paint on the waxed palette. The blending is done on the painting surface.

Fully load the brush into the dark value, gently tapping it onto the waxed palette. Fill in the rest of the dark value area. You have now basecoated the values and created the value changes. It will look choppy and unrefined, but that's okay!

Wash out your brush in the water basin. Remember to blot it on a paper towel, put it into the retarder and blot again.

When the painting surface is dry, with no shiny or wet spots, you may proceed to the next step.

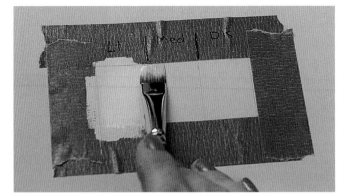

The left side of the brush has the light value and the right side has the medium value. Blend the values together, walking the brush back and forth between the two areas.

The first stage of value blocking will look choppy. You're working too hard if you're trying to get perfection at this stage.

Wet-on-Wet Blending and Refining

With a 1-inch (25mm) wash brush, moisten the painting surface with a generous amount of Retarder and Antiquing Medium. Extend the retarder beyond the painted area, brushing the retarder vertically, horizontally and in a crisscross fashion. Apply pressure to the brush, pushing the retarder into the pores of the paint to break the surface tension. Be patient and take the time to brush the surface with retarder for at least one minute.

While the surface is still glistening wet, dip the original blending brush (no. 10 blender) into the retarder and blot well on a paper towel. Repeat the original blending process, just as you did on the first coat. Hold your brush at a 33° angle and start with the light value. Move on to the medium value and blend through to the dark value, being more careful this time with your blending technique. You need to make sure this second layer of paint is a generous one.

While the surface is still wet, quickly clean the brush in water, removing all of the paint residue. Blot well on a paper towel, dip into the retarder and blot well again. With this clean brush at a 33° angle, refine your blending by very lightly brushing long strokes over the painting surface, moving from the light value area across the

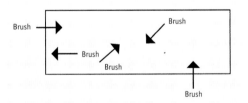

After the surface has been basecoated, brush in all directions to refine the values.

medium value to the dark value. It will appear that a lighter haze is moving across the surface, which is exactly what is happening. As you are refining, you are gently moving the second layer of values across the surface. To soften any brush marks during the refining stage, use very light, feathery brushstrokes. To move values or soften a harsh line between values, apply a bit more pressure.

You may clean the brush again, blot, dip into retarder, blot and continue the refining process as long as the surface is shiny. When the surface starts to take on a matte finish, you need to leave it alone or you might be in danger of lifting the paint.

You have now done acrylic blending! Remove the tape and see how you did. The process of acrylic blending works like this: Brushing retarder into the painted surface lightly softens the first layer of paint and makes the surface wet. When the next layer is added, the two layers join together for wet-on-wet blending. You need to add enough paint in the second layer so that it actually joins with the bottom layer and is not just skimming over the top.

It is my goal to blend an object in these two steps: basecoating with values, then wet-on-wet blending and refining. But what do you do if you are unhappy with the final results? First, dry the painting surface. You may speed-dry the surface with a hair dryer, but make sure the surface is back to room temperature before you apply any paint, retarder or mediums. If the surface is the slightest bit warm, any mediums or paint you apply will become sticky or tacky.

Reapply the retarder and repeat step two—wet-on-wet blending and refining. How many times can you repeat this step? As many times as needed. Just remember that after you have ten coats of paint, it will appear to be appliquéd, not painted. The goal is to do it in two steps.

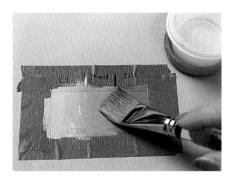

To reactivate the paint for wet-on-wet blending, brush retarder onto the first stage of the painting for at least one minute. Apply it with pressure to break down the surface tension.

With a generous second coat, reapply and blend all the values as before. This produces the wet-on-wet blending. Even after you have applied the second coat of wet-on-wet blending, some refining is still required.

Refine the blending with a clean brush that is slightly moistened with Retarder and Antiquing Medium, using light, feathery strokes.

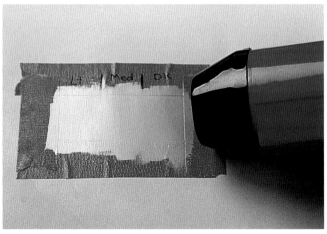

Holding the hair dryer as shown above allows the airflow to move across the surface, thus keeping any hot air from backing up into the dryer and burning it out. Any time a hair dryer is used to dry the surface, make sure the surface is back to room temperature before applying any paints or mediums.

This completes the blending and refining process. Once the tape has been removed, you can clean up any seepage with a cotton swab dipped in water.

CHAPTER FIVE

*H*ighlights, Shading and Shadows

Developing a painting is similar to getting dressed. First things first—underclothes, outer clothes, jewelry and final accessories. The same goes for a painting. Form is first and foremost in every painting. By taking your time and building the foundation one step at a time, the final outcome will be easier to achieve. Adding highlights and shading on top of a blended form gives added depth, dimension and realism to a still-life painting that cannot be accomplished in any other way. Adding these and other enhancements with purpose and color knowledge is what makes a good painting outstanding.

The enhancements discussed in this chapter are turning color, accents, highlights, shines, shading, reflected light, reflected color and cast shadows.

Turning Color

We know that as an object nears the light source, it gets lighter, brighter and warmer. As it recedes from the light source, it gets darker, duller and cooler. To ease the viewer's eye from the warm lights around an object to the cool darks, a turning color is placed where the medium and dark values come together. This also adds color harmony and coordination to the overall painting.

The turning color is normally a pure, warm, semitransparent to transparent color placed on the painted objects.

When placed on an object where the medium and dark values join together, the turning color takes a crescent shape. It takes a more triangular shape when it is placed on the edge of the object or container.

1 Apply pressure to the brush when blending out on the waxed palette until the turning color fades from semitransparent to transparent. Gradate the color across the entire brush.

2 Moisten the surface with Retarder and Antiquing Medium, then paint the turning color with more pigment in the center, fading out at the edges. In this case, the turning color is painted in a crescent shape.

3 Soften the turning color with a mop brush. Notice the accent color that has been placed on the spoon above. This helps tie in the pink details on the cup (see Accents, page 29, and project one, page 34).

Accents

Accents are usually pure color added to a dull area to give it some added attention. It is also another way to carry color throughout a design. Accents are most commonly placed on receding edges and are most effective if they don't change the value of the area on which they are placed. In the first project on page 34, the accents are the bits of pink placed on the receding edge of the spoon and tea bag.

Accents are applied in the same manner as turning color.

Highlights

There are different techniques for painting highlights and shading. We will look at each technique a step at a time.

Just as there is a value placement map for the placement of the mixed values for each project, there is also a glazing map for the placement of the highlights, shines, shading, reflected light, reflected color, and cast shadows.

Dry-Brush Method

Drybrushing means painting with a brush that is dry on a surface that is dry—thus the term "drybrush." Load the brush as shown in the steps at right. Apply this loaded brush to the highlight area of your painting, referring to the glazing map for each project. You should not go beyond the highlight or light value zone. The idea is to lightly touch the brush down in the center of the highlight area and move the brush in a circular motion while also moving up and down the highlight area. You should have more paint pigment in the center of the highlight and then softly fade at the outer edges.

Build each shine or highlight with progressively lighter values, referring to each project for highlight and shine colors. Pyramid the colors inside the first application, slowly building the values. The trick is to use almost no paint and to touch down at the same starting spot each time. Make sure to give it a bit of drying time between each layer of drybrushing, or you may dig a hole in your painting.

You may need to clean the colors from your brush from time to time. Do not rinse your brush in water. Put a small amount of Retarder and Antiquing Medium on a paper towel and wipe your brush clean. Then wipe the brush dry on a dry paper towel and let it dry a few minutes before continuing.

1 Dip the tips of the bristles of a dry mini stencil into the highlight value paint. Remove as much of the paint as possible on a paper towel.

2 Rub the brush in a circular motion on the waxed palette. Move the brush to different areas of the palette until it appears there is no paint on the brush.

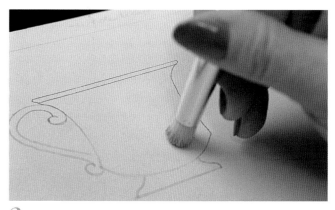

3 Touch the brush in the center of the highlight area. Work the brush in a circular motion, carefully brushing on the highlight. You may need to do several applications to achieve an even distribution of the paint. Be patient and take it slowly.

Flip-Float

With a large wash brush, moisten the painting surface with Retarder and Antiquing Medium. You will not be reactivating the paint because it is protected by Clear Glazing Medium, but you need to apply enough pressure to break down the surface tension. Side load the high side of an angle brush into the highlight shine mix, referring to each project for flip-float color mixes. Blend with pressure onto a waxed palette so that there is a strong edge of color on the high edge of the brush. Then follow the steps at right.

1 Dip one corner of an angular brush into the paint, then blend the color across the brush. The color should fade from strong, semitransparent to transparent.

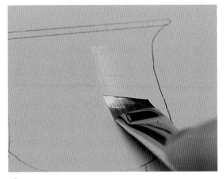

2 Holding the brush at a 33° angle, apply the strong edge of color to the center of the highlight area. Pull the brush down in the highlight area—the color will fade out to the right.

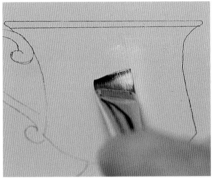

3 Flip the brush over and place the strong edge of color right next to the strong edge from the previous stroke. Pull the brush down in the highlight area—the color will fade out to the left.

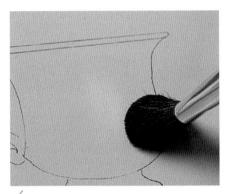

4 Soften the strokes by lightly dusting the whole area with a mop brush.

Shine

While the surface is still moist with retarder, reload the angle brush with a small corner load of the shine mix (refer to each project for the shine color). Apply this soft type of highlight following the steps at right.

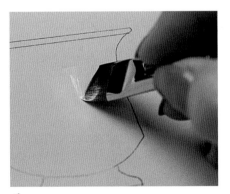

1 While the surface is still wet with retarder from the flip-float, reload the angle brush with a small float of paint. Paint a line in the center of the flip-float.

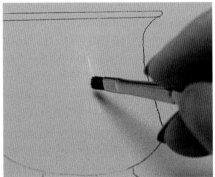

2 Soften the shine with a small mop brush so that it builds softly to a final highlight and doesn't look like a dot or spot.

Pat-Blending

Very often when painting round objects, such as fruit and flowers, I use the pat-blend method to paint a highlight.

For this method, moisten the painting surface with retarder. Using an angle brush that is appropriate for the size of the object, dip the brush into retarder and blot lightly onto a paper towel. Load the high end of the brush into the highlight mix. Now blend lightly on the waxed palette, using less pressure than you did for floated color. The paint should move only halfway across the brush, going from opaque to semitransparent. Holding the brush at a 33° angle, apply the paint to the center of the highlight area, lightly patting and blending while you move the brush in a complete circle. Soften the outer edges with a mop. While the surface is still moist with retarder, reload the angle brush with a very small corner load of the shine mix for that project. Apply a softer spot or dot in the center of the pat-blend. Tap around the outer edges of the dot with a small mop brush to soften and blend it in.

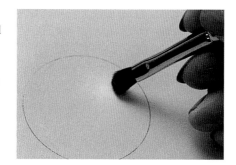

Soften the pat-blend with a small mop brush so the shine builds softly to a final highlight and doesn't look like a spot or dot.

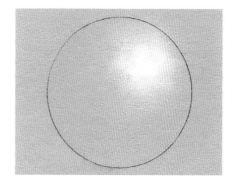

Remember, value follows form, so the drybrushing and pat-blending on a sphere will be round.

Shading

Reinforcing the shading will add extra depth to the painting. To do this, moisten the surface with Retarder and Antiquing Medium, making sure to carry the retarder onto the background area. Dip an angle brush in retarder, then load the high end of the brush into the shading mix, referring to each project for the shading mix. Blend it out on your waxed palette until the paint is semitransparent to transparent.

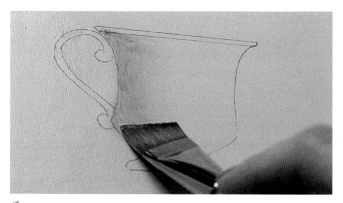

1 Paint the first shading so the color lightly fades toward the center where the medium and dark values meet.

2 Paint a second shading on top of the first, but do not extend the color as far into the center of the cup.

Apply this color to the reinforced shading area of your painting, referring to the glazing map for each project. Softly blend out the outer edges with a small mop brush. Several smaller shadings of progressively darker values may need to be applied. Soften each layer with a mop. If you have problems adding one layer of shading on top of another (stacking paint wet-on-wet), then let it dry between layers and remoisten the surface with retarder. If some of the shade color gets onto your background while mopping, simply remove it with a clean brush moistened with water.

Reflected Light

I refer to reflected light as a highlight in a shaded area. It occurs most frequently on cylinders and spheres, but may also appear on backgrounds and foregrounds. As I have stated before, I use an upper right-hand light source at an approximately 45° angle. We know that the light does not hit an object with a single beam but hits the front of the object that is closest to the light first—the highlight area. It then continues to radiate around the object, hitting somewhere on the background, such as on a table, wall or another object. The light then bounces back and will often catch on the edge of the cylinder or sphere in the shaded area, away from or opposite the light source.

Because the reflected light hits in a cool shaded area and is not as strong as the primary light (light in the highlight area), the reflected light will be a cool light. In most instances, this is accomplished by adding blue or a cool color pigment to a mix or white paint. Like the primary light, the reflected light has value changes and a brighter shine within it, but the reflected light will never be brighter than the primary light.

Like the flip-float, shine and shading, the reflected light is applied with an angle brush. It is loaded in the same manner and applied to a surface that has been premoistened with retarder. After the first application of the reflected light, soften with a mop brush. Then add the brighter shine of the reflected light and soften with a smaller mop.

Reflected Color

When an object that is very bright or shiny is placed next to a light object, or one that is reflective in nature, often the color of the first object will reflect onto the second object. An example of this is seen in the first project (see page 34). The shiny gold rim of the teacup reflects onto the silver spoon. This reflected color will also have value change and will be brighter the closer it is to the object.

Reflected color is applied onto a surface that has been premoistened with Retarder and Antiquing Medium in the same manner as turning colors and accents.

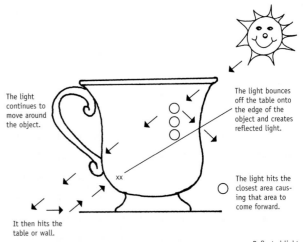

The light continues to move around the object.

The light bounces off the table onto the edge of the object and creates reflected light.

The light hits the closest area causing that area to come forward.

It then hits the table or wall.

xx = Reflected light

Cast Shadows

Shadow work gives the viewer information about the painting. It tells which direction the light is coming from, how close an object is to another object or surface and the contour of the object on which the shadow falls. The shadow falls opposite the light source. The closer an object is to another object, the darker the shadow. If an object casts a shadow onto a curved surface, the shadow will follow the curvature of that surface.

As with everything else in realistic painting, a shadow will have value change. It is darkest at the contact point and then fades out and becomes softly diffused at the outer edges.

To apply a shadow, moisten the surface with retarder. Load the high end of an angle brush with the shadow color. Blend well back and forth on a waxed palette, the same as you would for floated color.

Apply the shadow color onto the surface with the darkest edge at the contact point where the object touches the surface. Soften the outer edge with a mop. You may need several applications to achieve the desired depth.

Cast Shadows
The shadow from the knife follows the curvature of the apple, telling the viewer that the apple is round. The shadow straightens out when it reaches the table, telling the viewer that the surface is flat.

Shadow Theory

1. In order for a shadow to be present, there must be a light source.

2. A shadow will always fall opposite the light source.

3. There must be a surface or something to receive the shadow.

4. A shadow will follow the contour of the object or area that receives the shadow. For example: The photo of the shadow from the knife follows the curvature of the apple and then straightens out when it hits the surface of the table.

5. Even though a shadow is transparent, it will have a value change. It will be darkest where the object touches the surface, and lighter, softer and more transparent along the outer edges, forming a halo of light.

An Overview of the Process

1. Form is always first, so to begin, basecoat in values, then blend wet-on-wet and refine.

2. Turning color and accents are added next and are placed onto a surface that is premoistened with Retarder and Antiquing Medium.

3. Before painting the decoration and detail, seal the surface with Clear Glazing Medium. Seal again after the decoration is painted and dry.

4. Enhancements, which include highlights, shines, shading, reflected light and reflected color, are all applied to a surface that is premoistened with Retarder and Antiquing Medium. The exception is drybrushing, which is applied to a dry surface. All enhancements are placed on top of any decoration and detail.

5. Cast shadows are added last and are placed on a surface that is premoistened with Retarder and Antiquing Medium.

Tea with Edith

Practical application or hands-on learning is the easiest way to actually learn and retain the previous lessons. This first piece is designed specifically to put into practice color theory and blending techniques. The wooden tea box holds flavored varieties as well as regular cut teas. This piece was created for my loving mother-in-law, Edith DeRenzo.

Materials

Silver Brush Ltd. Brushes
no. 2 5020S Chisel Blender
no. 8 5020S Chisel Blender
no. 10 5020S Chisel Blender
⅛-inch (3mm) 5319S Wee Mop
¼-inch (6mm) 5319S Wee Mop
no. 8 5019S Refining Mop
1-inch (25mm) 2008S Square Wash
1-inch (25mm) 2514S Wash
    for varnishing
no. 20/0 2407S Ultra Mini Script Liner
no. 0 2522S Monogram Liner
⅛-inch (3mm) 5006S
    Blending Floating Angular
¼-inch (6mm) 5006S
    Blending Floating Angular
½-inch (12mm) 5006S
    Blending Floating Angular
no. 2 1721S Stencil Mini

Jo Sonja's Chroma Acrylics
Titanium White (TW)
Unbleached Titanium (UT)
Cadmium Yellow Lt (CYL)
Cadmium Yellow Mid (CYM)
Yellow Deep (YD)
Gold Oxide (GO)
Raw Sienna (RS)
Brown Earth (BE)
Burnt Umber (BU)
Ultra Blue Deep (UB)
Pthalo Blue (PthB)
Permanent Alizarine (PA)
Background Color
Cashmere

Jo Sonja's Mediums
All Purpose Sealer
Flow Medium
Retarder and Antiquing Medium
Clear Glazing Medium
Gloss varnish
Matte varnish

Additional Supplies
general materials listed in chapter one

Surface
from The Cutting Edge

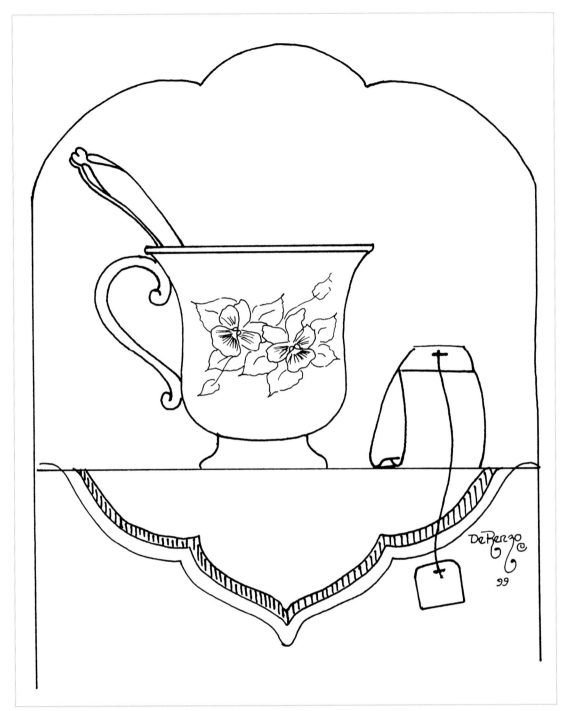

Background Preparation

1 Fill any nail holes or wood joints with Jo Sonja's Water Based Wood Filler. Allow to dry one hour, then sand to a refined finish. Wipe down and remove the dust with a lint-free cloth. Prepare a mix of two parts Cashmere to one part All Purpose Sealer (2:1).

This is the background color. Now prepare another mix of seven parts of the background mix you just created and one part Flow Medium (7:1). Mix well with a palette knife and apply to the surface with a 1-inch (25mm) wash brush.

2 Wet Sanding

After the Cashmere background mix has been applied and the surface is dry, you're ready to wet sand. Wet sanding removes raised wood grain and painting ridges, and gives you a smoother, more refined painting surface. Lightly dip the wet and dry sandpaper into water and gently apply it to the painted surface in small circular motions. Re-dip the sandpaper into water when necessary. Don't get nervous when this appears to be messy, because it is. Don't touch it—just let it dry. Trust me, it's all right.

When the surface is dry, paint it again with the 1-inch (25mm) wash brush and dry. Lightly buff the entire surface with a piece of brown paper bag.

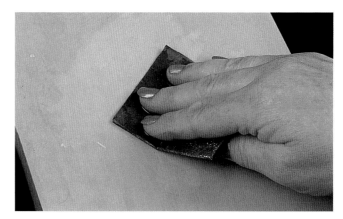

Step 2 Wet sand the surface.

3 The Eggshell Finish

Using a sponge roller loaded with the background mix, apply an eggshell finish to the entire painting surface, using the technique described on page 18. Dry and lightly sand again.

4 The Second Background Color

Measure 1⅜ inches (3.5cm) up from the top of the base of the piece. Use your graph ruler to measure from the bottom edge to ensure your table line is not slanted and is perfectly horizontal. Place a piece of painter's tape across the top edge of the table line.

Mix Cashmere + Brown Earth + Burnt Umber for the dark background mix, and paint the area below the tape using the 1-inch (25mm) wash brush. Apply two coats, drying and sanding between coats. Remove the tape.

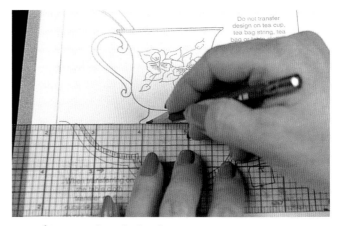

Step 6 Trace and verify the design.

5 The Background Trim

With white transfer paper and a pencil, transfer just the decorative border (see the pattern on page 36) to the surface, centering it horizontally. Mix a value in between the background mix and the dark background mix for the medium background mix. Use this to paint the trim area around the design, the sides of the box and the lid of the box. See the illustration at right for guidance.

Tip

Always save some of your mixed background color for any touch-ups. Empty film containers work well for storing mixed paint.

6 Tracing and Proving the Design

Trace the design with a pencil onto tracing paper, using a graph ruler for straight lines.

Background Color Placement

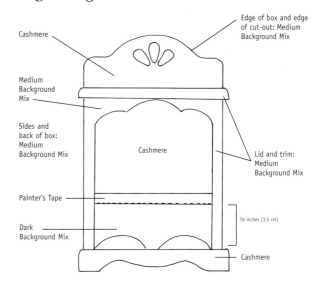

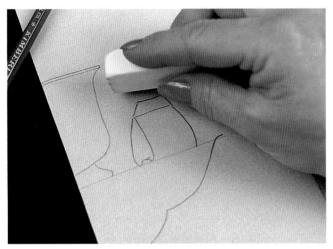

7 To make sure the cup is in exact proportion to itself, fold the tracing paper in half with the pencil side facing out and match the right side of the cup with the left side. Do they match? Probably not. Decide which side looks correct, then erase the incorrect side and retrace it so that both sides match. Now trace the rest of the design using the folded line down the center of the cup as the vertical control.

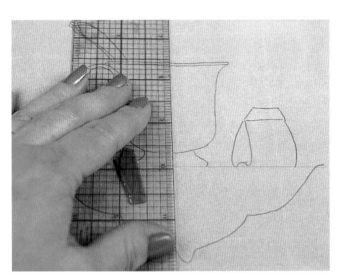

8 Place the bottom edge of a graph ruler on the horizontal surface. Slide the pattern under the graph ruler. Line up the vertical folded line of the pattern with the vertical lines of the ruler. This allows you to make sure the cup is perpendicular to the horizontal plane. Slide the transfer paper under the design (shiny side down), and carefully retrace only the teacup and tea bag. Use only enough pressure to transfer the pattern, not to leave pencil grooves in the wood. Do not transfer the tablecloth or any of the flowers or detail at this time. Place a piece of painter's tape across the top rim of the teacup and another piece under the foot of the cup.

Value Blending and Refining

This first project is an eye-level perspective, high-key painting. High key means that the largest percentage of the values used in the painting range from a medium value up to a highlight value. This doesn't mean that the lower values aren't used; it means that they are used sparingly and as only a small percentage of the overall painting. In fact, the proper use of the darker values in a high-key painting is what gives the painting dimension and brings it to life.

The background color, Cashmere, is a light value, warm in temperature and considered a neutral color in the orange family. For the medium trim and table values, I chose to lower the value of Cashmere with the earth color Brown Earth—a red-orange neighbor to the orange Cashmere. I further deepened and toned with the earth color Burnt Umber, keeping the three values warm and neutral.

Next, a color is needed for the teacup that is warmer and lighter than the background so the cup comes forward to the viewer. I chose Unbleached Titanium, a yellow-orange neighbor to the orange Cashmere, for the base color.

Brown Earth and Burnt Umber are again used to tone and lower the values, thus keeping color harmony throughout the painting. A warm black is mixed for the darkest values and darker glazing. Compared to the rest of the colors in the teacup, this black is quite cool and will push areas painted with it into the background.

9 Teacup and Tea Bag

Mix the teacup and tea bag values below and follow steps 10 through 23 for painting the cup. When complete, basecoat the handle with the medium value and create roundness by shading with the dark and low dark values.

Teacup and Tea Bag
Unbleached Titanium, Raw Sienna, Brown Earth, Burnt Umber, Ultra Blue Deep.
- Warm Black: BU + UB = WB mix
- Medium: UT + RS + BE + tad BU
- Light: Medium mix + UT + tad RS
- Highlight: UT + light mix + tech RS
- Dark: Medium mix + BE + BU
- Low Dark: Dark mix + tad WB mix

Note: tad = small amount; tech = less than a tad

Hi Lt	Lt	Med	Dark	Lo Dk

Value Placement Map

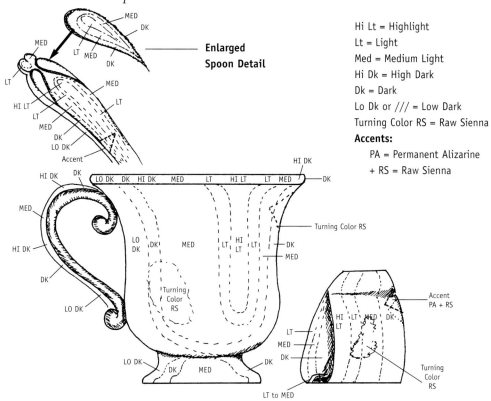

Enlarged
Spoon Detail

Hi Lt = Highlight
Lt = Light
Med = Medium Light
Hi Dk = High Dark
Dk = Dark
Lo Dk or /// = Low Dark
Turning Color RS = Raw Sienna

Accents:
   PA = Permanent Alizarine
   + RS = Raw Sienna

Tip

When mixing values, I often test the colors on a piece of manila folder that has been painted with the background color to see how well the mixed value settles onto the background.

10 To begin basecoating the values on the teacup, dip the no. 10 blender into retarder.

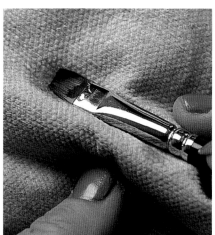

11 Blot the brush on a paper towel to remove any excess retarder.

12 Load the brush fully into the highlight value.

13 Gently tap the brush onto the waxed palette to remove excess paint and to push the paint into the bristles.

14 Hold the brush at a 33° angle to the painting surface and fill in the highlight area. Stretch the value beyond the highlight value zone so that you can blend the light value back into it.

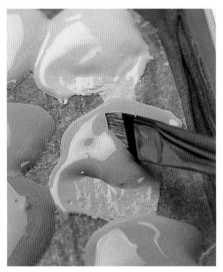

15 Side load the brush into the light value mix, but do not add any more retarder.

16 Place half of the brush into the highlight area and half of the brush onto the light value area, just as you did in the blending exercise. Blend the two values on the surface, creating a mid-value between the two. Remember that value follows form, so manipulate the brush as you round the corner at the bottom where the two values curve.

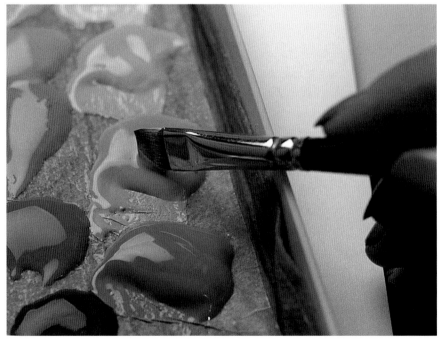

17 Once you have blended the highlight and light areas together, you are ready to blend the light and medium values. To do this, the highlight value needs to be removed from the brush. Side load the side of the brush that has the highlight value into the medium value paint puddle.

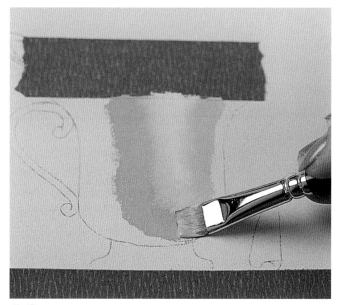

18 Place the half of the brush with the light value paint onto the light value area and the half of the brush with the medium value paint onto the medium value area. Blend the two values, moving the brush back and forth between the light and medium values to soften the hard edges. Again, turn the brush or painting surface as you round the bottom.

19 Once you have blended the light and medium values together, fully load the brush into the medium value paint.

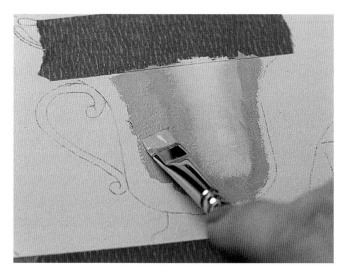

20 Fill in the medium value area of the teacup. The medium value, or body color, is used on the largest area of any painting object. Remember to keep the brush at a 33° angle.

21 Side load the brush into the dark value and start blending the medium and dark values together. When blending smaller areas like the right side of the cup, put more pressure on the right side of the brush and lift up the left side. Keep the brush at the 33° angle. When blending the medium and dark values on the left side, continue with the regular blending technique.

22 To begin blending the dark and low dark values, side load the side of the brush with medium value paint and place into the low dark value.

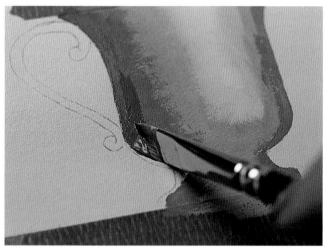

23 Continue to blend the far left side of the cup. This time apply more pressure on the left side of the brush, lifting up on the right side. Carefully stroke in the left side and left bottom curve, blending the dark and low dark values together. You have now completed basecoating the cup in values. Let the surface dry completely with no shiny or wet spots.

24 Gold Trim

When the teacup is thoroughly dry, place tape across the bottom edge of the gold trim for easier painting. Basecoat the gold trim in the same way, following the value placement guide. Make sure the highlight of the gold trim matches up with the highlight of the teacup. If you dried the surface with a hair dryer, make sure the wood is cool before removing the tape, or the glue from the tape will remain on the painted surface. Basecoat the tea bag, as well, using the teacup values.

Gold Trim
Raw Sienna, Cadmium Yellow Mid, Gold Oxide, Brown Earth, Burnt Umber
- Medium: RS + CYM
- Light: Medium mix + CYM
- Highlight: CYM + tad light mix
- High Dark: Medium mix + GO
- Dark: High dark mix + BE
- Low Dark: Dark mix + BU

Hi Lt	Lt	Med	Hi Dk	Dark	Lo Dk

25 Spoon

I wanted the spoon to be silver, which converts to values of gray when painted. The silver grays need to be quite warm so they settle and rest quietly against the warm background color, but they also need to be distinguishable from the grays of the cup. I chose Titanium White as the base color and grayed it with the Warm Black mix, then warmed it with the neutral yellow-orange Raw Sienna. Basecoat the spoon, following value placement map.

Spoon
Titanium White, Raw Sienna
- Medium: TW + RS + WB mix
- Light: Medium mix + TW + RS
- Highlight: Light mix + TW + tech RS
- Dark: Medium mix + WB mix
- Low Dark: Dark mix + WB mix

Hi Lt	Lt	Med	Dark	Lo Dk

26 At this point, all the elements have been basecoated with values. Remember, the elements will not be perfectly blended at this stage. Choppy is okay—you're striving for change and solid coverage.

27 Wet-on-Wet Blending and Refining

After all the elements have been basecoated and are completely dry, proceed with step two of blending: wet-on-wet blending and refining. Tape off the edges of the cup again, and reactivate the paint with retarder as described on page 26. Paint a generous second layer of values on the teacup, then clean the brush, dip it in retarder and refine the blending. Refer to page 26 for the complete steps for wet-on-wet blending and refining.

28 When you're satisfied with the blending on the teacup, gently pull off the tape and repeat these steps for the gold trim, tea bag and spoon.

29 When you're done with all of the refined blending, clean the brush with water and clean up any paint on the background area. If the paint is too dry and can't be removed with water, dry the surface and do any touch up with the background color. Let the surface dry until there are no shiny or wet spots. You are now ready to proceed to turning color, details and decoration.

30 Turning Color

When the painting surface is dry, use a 1-inch (25mm) wash brush to moisten the surface with retarder. You are not trying to reactivate the surface, but you do want to apply enough pressure to break down the surface tension. Make sure to moisten the entire surface, including the outside edges of the background. Having retarder on the surface will enable the paint to become transparent and moveable.

31 The turning color for this project is Raw Sienna. I chose Raw Sienna because it is a pure warm yellow-orange that coordinates with the overall color scheme, carrying the yellow gold trim on the cup and handle through the painting.

Place Raw Sienna onto the wet palette. Now take a ½-inch (12mm) angular brush, dip it into retarder, blot well onto a paper towel and load the high end of the brush into the Raw Sienna.

Step 26 Here all the values have been basecoated.

Step 31 Load the brush with the turning color.

32 Blend the brush back and forth onto the waxed palette, using pressure to cause the paint to move across the bristles of the brush. The pigment should be semi-transparent at the high end of the bristles and become more transparent as it moves across the brush. The brush is now loaded for floated color.

Step 32 Blend the paint across the brush.

33 Refer to the value placement map on page 39 for where to place the turning color. Holding the brush at a 33° angle, apply the paint to the crescent shape, softly patting around the edges. With the brush loaded and blended in the same manner, apply the paint to the edge of the cup, softly blending it in a triangular shape.

34 While the surface is still wet, take a dry no. 8 refining mop and further soften the outer edges of both shapes, much in the same way that you would soften cheek rouge.

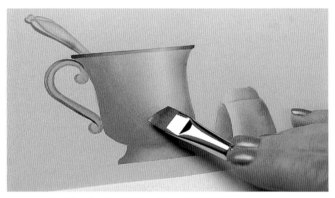

Step 33 Apply the turning color to the cup.

35 Apply the turning color with Permanent Alizarine for the gold rim and Permanent Alizarine + Raw Sienna for the tea bag.

36 Accent
To carry the pinkish reds of the flowers through the design, place accents of Permanent Alizarine + Raw Sienna on the receding edge of the spoon and tea bag. Moisten the surface with Retarder and Antiquing Medium. Apply the accents in the same manner as the turning color. Refer to the value placement map on page 39 for the exact placement of the accents.

37 Remove Graphite Lines
Before adding any decorations, remove any graphite lines with Archival Odorless Solvent. To do this, moisten a lint-free cloth with the solvent and gently rub out the lines. If the lines are not coming off, add more solvent on the cloth. Remove the excess solvent residue with a clean cloth. Let the painting surface dry completely.

Step 34 Soften the color with a mop brush.

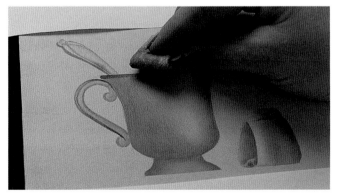

Step 37 Remove graphite lines before sealing.

38 Clear Glazing Medium

Sealing the painting surface with one coat of Clear Glazing Medium adds extra depth to the painting and protects all of your work to this point. If you make a mistake while painting any decoration or detail, it can be removed with a cotton swab or soft rag and water without disturbing the painting underneath. Once Clear Glazing Medium has been applied to the surface, you can no longer reactivate the paint underneath with Retarder and Antiquing Medium.

To apply Clear Glazing Medium, use a dry 1-inch (25mm) wash brush. Brush on a smooth, even, undiluted coat. Cover the entire painting surface, even the bottom half. When first applied it will appear a bit milky, but it dries clear within five to ten minutes. You may also speed-dry with a hair dryer. When the surface is dry, it will appear slightly glossy. Don't worry—it will disappear when varnished.

Be sure to wash your brush immediately afterward with soap and water.

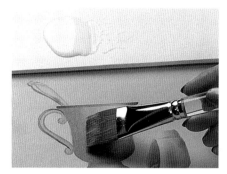

Step 38 Seal with Clear Glazing Medium.

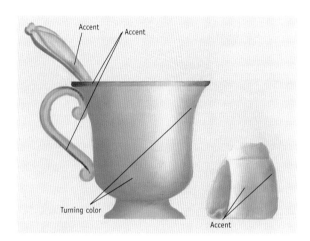

Decoration

39
When the surface is dry and not the least bit tacky, transfer the violets and tablecloth patterns onto the surface with white transfer paper. Do not transfer the detail for the cloth.

40 Flower Design

Because the background, teacup and tea bag are neutral in color, the flower designs draw attention and brighten up the painting while still being harmonious with the overall color scheme. The two new colors that are introduced are Yellow Deep, a yellow-orange with an intensity of 1, and Permanent Alizarine, a red-violet with the intensity of 4. Both of these colors are of a high or bright intensity and demand the attention that is needed. To make sure these new colors are in harmony with each other and the rest of the painting, they are mixed with each other and with Unbleached Titanium, the "mother" or background color because it is the main base color of the teacup. Warm Black is used to tone and shade the dark colors, keeping them consistent with the rest of the painting. The leaves are painted a grayed green using color already included in the palette. Rouging was added to soften the flowers.

Moisten the surface with retarder, then lightly basecoat the violets and leaves. Dry the surface and remove the graphite lines from the flower design. Some of the paint might also come off where the graphite lines were, leaving an empty line. Do any touch up at this time before you continue completing the design.

Yellow Violets
Yellow Deep, Unbleached Titanium, Permanent Alizarine, Burnt Umber, Ultra Blue Deep, Pthalo Blue

Front Petal
- Warm Black: BU + UB = WB mix
- Base: YD
- Highlight: UT + tech YD
- Shade: YD + PA + tech BU

Back Petals
- Base: PA + tad WB mix = Dark Red (DR) mix
- Highlight: UT + tad UB + tech PthB

| Base | Hi Lt | Shade | Base | Hi Lt |

Pink Violet
- Base: PA + UT + YD
- Highlight: UT + tech pink violet base mix
- Shade: PA + WB mix (same as base mix for back two petals of yellow violets)

Base   Hi Lt   Shade

Gather Lines
PA + WB mix (darker than DR mix)

Violet Centers
WB mix + PA

Mustache
UT + tech YD

Gather   Centers   Mustache
lines

Rouging Around Design
Base leaf mix
Raw Sienna

Leaves
Yellow Deep, Unbleached Titanium, Ultra Blue Deep, Pthalo Blue
- Base: YD + WB mix + tad UB + tad UT + tech PthB
- Shade: Base leaf mix + WB mix + YD + tech PthB
- Leaf liner: Leaf shade mix

Base   Shade

41 Now that the flowers and leaves are basecoated, moisten the surface again with Retarder and Antiquing Medium and continue with the highlights and shading. Apply the rouging to the surface that is moistened with Retarder and Antiquing Medium and then soften with a mop.

42 Tablecloth
Up to this point we have been painting solid objects, like the teacup, by blending in stages. First, when the surface was dry, the values were basecoated. Then the surface was moistened with retarder and wet-on-wet blending and refining were done.

However, the tablecloth for this project is semitransparent, not completely solid. Any time transparency is desired, Retarder and Antiquing Medium needs to be

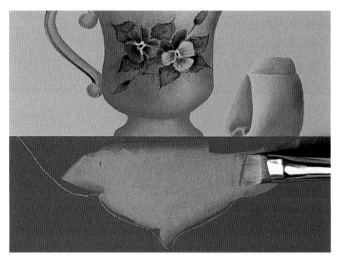

Step 42 Paint a wash over the tablecloth area.

Step 43 Soften the paint with a mop brush.

applied to the surface. Not only does this make the paint pigment semitransparent to transparent—depending on how much pigment is applied to the wet surface—but it also enables the paint to be moveable and the refine blending to be accomplished with a mop.

To paint the tablecloth, moisten the surface with Retarder and Antiquing Medium. Using the ½-inch (12mm) angular brush, brush-mix the medium teacup mix and the dark teacup mix with retarder onto a waxed palette until you have a semitransparent wash of color. Apply this semitransparent wash as evenly as possible over the entire tablecloth, including the cutout area.

43 While the surface is still wet, blend and soften any lines or brushstrokes with the no. 8 refining mop. Don't worry about going outside the design lines.

44 Before the surface dries, moisten a no. 2 chisel blender with water and remove the paint over the cutout area. You may need to redampen the brush several times to clean out the area sufficiently. If this wipe-out technique does not work for you, then dry the surface and paint out the cutout area using the dark background mix and a no. 2 chisel blender.

45 Using a larger brush in the same manner, create a clean sharp edge for the outside of the tablecloth.

46 When the cloth is dry, remove the graphite lines, wipe off any excess residue, then paint the cloth detail using the light teacup mix and a no. 20/0 script liner brush. Add a little shading detail using dark teacup mix.

47 Tea Bag Details

Complete the details for the tea bag using the mixes listed below.

Tag
Pink violets base mix + tad dark background mix

Writing on Tag
Dark red violet mix

String
Highlight teacup mix

Staples
- Base: Low dark spoon mix
- Highlight: Highlight spoon mix
- Shade: WB

48 Sealing

When all of the decorations and details are completed and dried, apply one coat of Clear Glazing Medium to the entire surface and let dry.

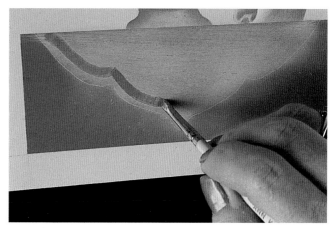

Step 44 Remove the cutout area with water.

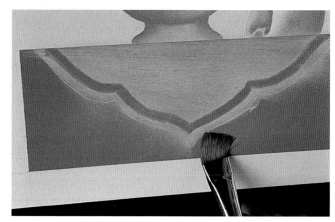

Step 45 Clean up the edge of the cloth with water.

Highlights, Shading and Shadows

49 You have created form, added turning colors and accents, and decorated the form. You are now ready to enhance the painting. Again, seal off the painting surface with one coat of Clear Glazing Medium, making it mistake-proof and adding depth. Let this dry. Remember, just as you have been working in values to create the form when blending, values are also used when adding highlights and shading and they follow the same rules.

Glazing Map

oooo = Highlights
⁰🙼 = Shines
//// = Shading
xxxxx = Darker shading
⋰⋱⋰ = Reflected light
⋰•⋱ = Shine on reflected light

50 Teacup

Highlights
Apply over the flower design to unify it with the cup.

1. Drybrush on the highlight teacup mix.
2. Drybrush on Unbleached Titanium.
3. Flip-float on Unbleached Titanium + Titanium White.
4. Add a final shine of Titanium White + tech Cadmium Yellow Mid (= Warm White).

Shading
1. Low dark teacup mix + Warm Black
2. Warm Black
3. More Warm Black

Reflected Light
1. Ultra Blue Deep + Titanium White + Pthalo Blue
2. First mix + more Titanium White

 Tip

Remember, drybrushing is done on a dry surface using a dry brush. All other glazing is done on a surface that has been moistened with Retarder and Antiquing Medium. Review chapter five if needed.

51 Gold Trim

Highlight on Rim
1. Highlight gold trim mix
2. Cadmium Yellow Mid
3. Cadmium Yellow Lt
4. Dot shine: Titanium White + tad Cadmium Yellow Lt

Highlight on Handle
1. Light gold trim mix
2. Highlight gold trim mix
3. Yellow Deep
4. Dot shine: Cadmium Yellow Mid

Shading and Reflected Light
1. Same colors as on the teacup

52 Tea Bag

Highlight on Front Edge
1. Moisten surface with retarder and highlight using the highlight teacup mix.
2. Unbleached Titanium + Titanium White
3. Warm White (= Titanium White + tad Cadmium Yellow Mid)

Highlight on Back Edge
I used a temperature change in order for the back edge of the tea bag to show up and not fade into the background, yet not be as bright and light as the front edge.
1. Highlight teacup mix
2. Unbleached Titanium + Titanium White + tad Ultra Blue Deep

Shade on Right Edge
1. Low dark teacup mix
2. Low dark teacup mix + Warm Black mix

Shade on Inside Fold
1. Low dark teacup mix
2. Low dark teacup mix + Warm Black mix
3. Warm Black mix
4. More Warm Black mix

53 Spoon

Highlight
1. Highlight spoon mix
2. Highlight spoon mix + Titanium White + tad Raw Sienna
3. Flip-float with Titanium White + tad Raw Sienna.
4. Shine with the flip-float mix.

Shade
1. Low dark spoon mix + Warm Black mix
2. Warm Black mix

54 All Reflected Light
1. Ultra Blue Deep + Titanium White + tech Pthalo Blue
2. First mix + more Titanium White

55 All Reflected Color
1. Light gold trim mix
2. Shine: Highlight gold trim mix

56 All Cast Shadows
Paint all of the cast shadows with the Warm Black mix. The shadows will be darkest at the contact point and lightly fade out and become diffused at the outer edges. The contact points are under the teacup, tea bag and on the spoon next to the teacup.

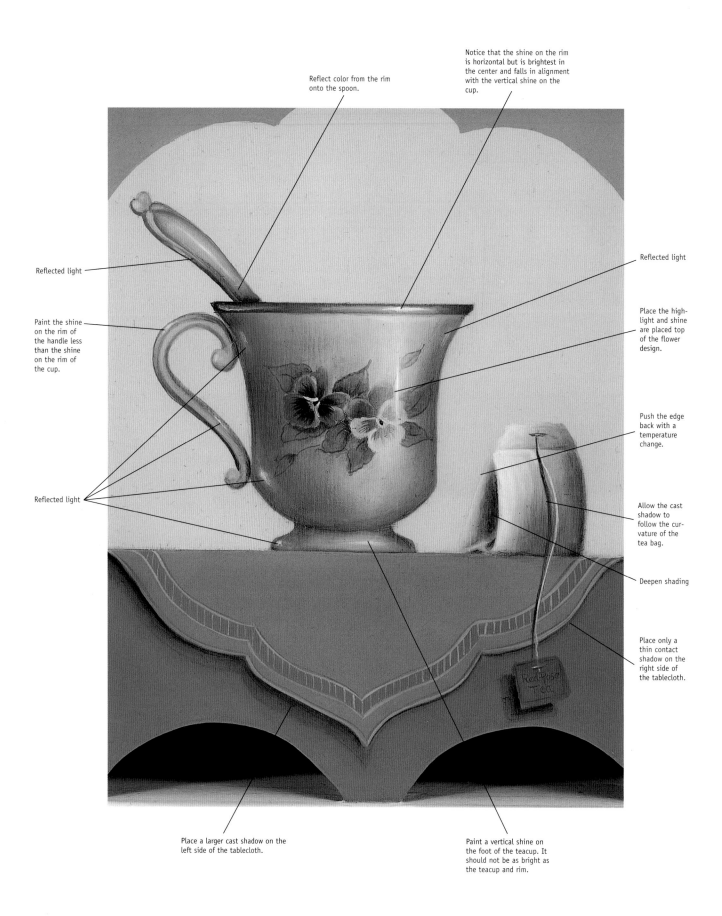

Reflect color from the rim onto the spoon.

Notice that the shine on the rim is horizontal but is brightest in the center and falls in alignment with the vertical shine on the cup.

Reflected light

Place the highlight and shine are placed top of the flower design.

Reflected light

Paint the shine on the rim of the handle less than the shine on the rim of the cup.

Push the edge back with a temperature change.

Reflected light

Allow the cast shadow to follow the curvature of the tea bag.

Deepen shading

Place only a thin contact shadow on the right side of the tablecloth.

Place a larger cast shadow on the left side of the tablecloth.

Paint a vertical shine on the foot of the teacup. It should not be as bright as the teacup and rim.

57 Trim Lines

Paint the trim on the top and bottom edges of the tea box with the dark background mix using the no. 20/0 script liner.

58 Varnishing

All of my paintings are done using Jo Sonja's Chroma Acrylics with the use of Retarder and Antiquing Medium. Because they are open-bodied paints containing no sealer, they take two to three weeks to dry and cure. With the addition of Retarder and Antiquing Medium, it can sometimes take longer. If you are anything like me, you don't have time to wait to varnish a project. I need it finished now! So to overcome this waiting period, I have found a solution:

When your painting is finished, heat-set it with a hair dryer. Blow a gentle stream of hot air across the surface. Be careful not to heat one area too much as it may bring any trapped-in sap up to the surface. But do get the surface quite warm so that you start the curing process. Allow the piece to cool to room temperature so there's not a hint of warmth.

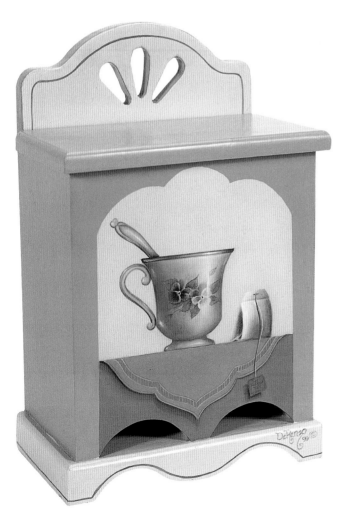

59

Apply one coat of Clear Glazing Medium. This not only seals the paint, but it also makes the varnish a little easier to apply. Heat-set with the hair dryer again and allow it to dry overnight. If the surface feels tacky in the morning, heat-set with the hair dryer again and let it cool! Then wipe the surface clean with a lint-free cloth, not a tack cloth.

60

For my personal preference, the matte varnish has too much matting agent and the gloss varnish is too shiny or glossy, so I find it necessary to mix the two. You can vary the levels of sheen in the gloss varnish with the amount of matte varnish you mix in. Play around until you find the formula that suits your personal preference. My favorite is equal parts matte and gloss varnish.

Before mixing the two together, gently shake or roll the containers to ensure even suspension and mixing of the matting and glossing agents. Do not thin the varnishes with water at any time. If needed, add Flow Medium instead. Mix only enough for your project, using a small clean bottle or film container. It will stay fresh for a few weeks but not much longer, as the mixture tends to separate and harden at the bottom.

61

Use a clean, dry varnish brush, not one that is damp or wet because water may cause streaking in the varnish. I have found the 1-inch (25mm) wash to be the best brush for varnishing; it allows the varnish to flow on easily and leaves no brush marks.

Apply the varnish using small, slip-slap or crisscross strokes, followed by long smoothing strokes in the direction of the wood grain. Reapply one more coat as soon as the first coat is dry to the touch. Allow the second coat to dry eight to ten hours or overnight. Between coats, wrap the brush in plastic wrap or a baggie.

62 Finishing

Lightly buff the surface with Super Film until it has a complete matte finish, remove the dust and apply two more coats of the varnish mixture. Let this dry to the touch. Sand with Super Film and apply two more coats. Six coats of varnish will make your piece alcohol resistant.

PROJECT 2

Love Letters

This project is dedicated to my dad and mom, Dave and Julie. When my mother passed away, one of the things I inherited was a box of love letters that my father sent to my mother while he was a marine during World War II. This box of letters gave me insight into a young man and woman who were in love during a time when our country was in the turmoil of war. It is my desire that when you finish painting this canvas stationery box, you will fill it with letters of your own history and heritage.

This beginning trompe l'oeil (pronounced "tromp loy," it literally means "that which deceives the eye") should be displayed on a coffee table or dresser, or placed wherever the viewer may look down at the painting.

Materials

Silver Brush Ltd. Brushes

no. 2 5020S Chisel Blender
no. 4 5020S Chisel Blender
no. 14 5020S Chisel Blender
⅛-inch (3mm) 5006S
    Blending Floating Angular
¼-inch (6mm) 5006S
    Blending Floating Angular
no. 20/0 2407S Ultra Mini Script Liner
no. 8 5019S Refining Mop
⅛-inch (3mm) 5319S Wee Mop
¼-inch (6mm) 5319S Wee Mop
1-inch (25mm) 2008S Square Wash
1-inch (25mm) 2514S Square Wash
    for varnishing

Jo Sonja's Chroma Acrylics

Titanium White (TW)
Cadmium Yellow Mid (CYM)
Raw Sienna (RS)
Burnt Umber (BU)
Unbleached Titanium (UT)
Permanent Alizarine (PA)
Paynes Grey (PG)
Ultra Blue Deep (UB)
Carbon Black (CB)
Iridescent Blue (IB)
Background Color
Cashmere

Jo Sonja's Mediums

All Purpose Sealer
Retarder and Antiquing Medium
Clear Glazing Medium
Flow Medium
Gloss varnish
Matte varnish

Additional Supplies

general materials listed in chapter one
old toothbrush

Surface

by Dalee, supplied by Viking
Woodcrafts, Inc.

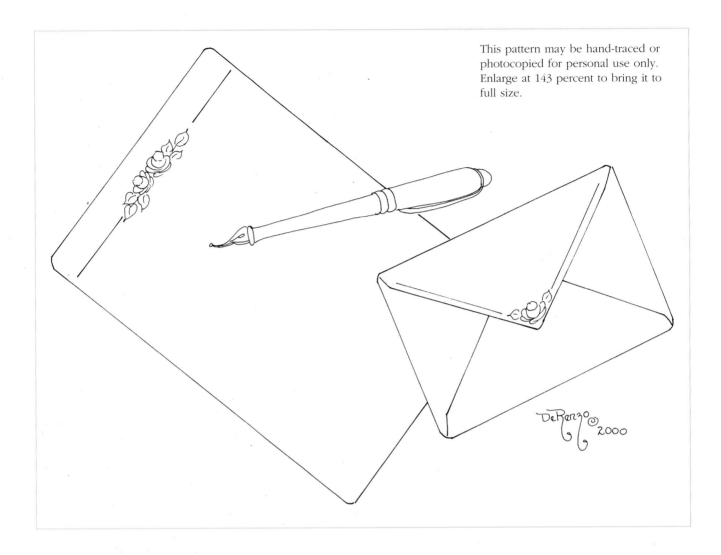

This pattern may be hand-traced or photocopied for personal use only. Enlarge at 143 percent to bring it to full size.

Background Preparation

1 Sand the canvas box well and remove any sanding dust. Mix Cashmere with Raw Sienna (1:1). To two parts of this mix, add one part All Purpose Sealer (2:1). Finally, to seven parts of the paint and sealer mix, add one part Flow Medium (7:1). Mix this well with the palette knife. Basecoat the entire box with this mix using the 1-inch (25mm) square wash. Apply three coats, sanding between coats.

2 When the surface is dry, transfer just the outline of the stationery and envelope. Place painter's tape around the outside perimeter of the stationery and envelope.

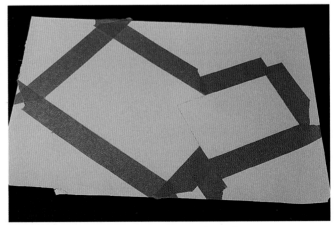

Step 2 Tape around the stationery and envelope.

3 Basecoat the stationery and envelope with solid coverage using a mix of Unbleached Titanium, Raw Sienna and Burnt Umber (1:1:1). This is the stationery mix.

4 Trace the outline of the stationery and envelope onto tracing paper and then cut out the shape. Take the tracing paper with the design cut out of it and tack it down to the box so that only the painted stationery and envelope show through. You are now ready to spatter and add the decoration to the stationery and envelope.

5 Spatter Colors

On your palette, prepare one puddle of paint of each of the following: Permanent Alizarine and Raw Sienna (1:1); Raw Sienna; Paynes Grey; and Burnt Umber. Add enough Retarder and Antiquing Medium to each of these colors so they are a bit soupy.

7 Quickly wipe the excess paint off the toothbrush onto a paper towel and then proceed to the next color. Repeat this process until you have a variation of colors and spatter marks on the stationery and envelope.

6 Lightly moisten the surface of the stationery and envelope with Retarder and Antiquing Medium. Take an old toothbrush and dip the bristles into one of the spattering colors. Shake the excess paint onto a paper towel. With the bristles of the toothbrush facing toward the painted surface, rub your thumbnail across the bristles so tiny spatters appear on the painted surface.

8 While the surface is still moist, take your 1-inch (25mm) mop brush and gently pounce up and down on the spatters to soften. Remove the tracing paper from the outer perimeter and wipe away any spatters that got on the background color. Dry the surface with a hair dryer.

9 Rose Design

Basecoat the rose design on the stationery and envelope, then shade and highlight using the colors below.

Rose Design
Permanent Alizarine, Raw Sienna, Burnt Umber, Unbleached Titanium, Cadmium Yellow Mid
- Base: Stationery mix + tad PA + tad RS
- Shade: Rose mix + PA + BU
- Highlight: UT + CYM = Warm White

Note: tad = small amount; tech = less than a tad

Base   Shade   Hi Lt

1. Basecoat using the ⅛-inch (3mm) angular brush.
2. Side load the brush with shading mix. Shade the inside and bottom of the bowl of the rose. Shade the inner edges of the petals.
3. Side load the brush with the highlight mix. Highlight the front and back edges of the bowl and the outer edges of the petals.

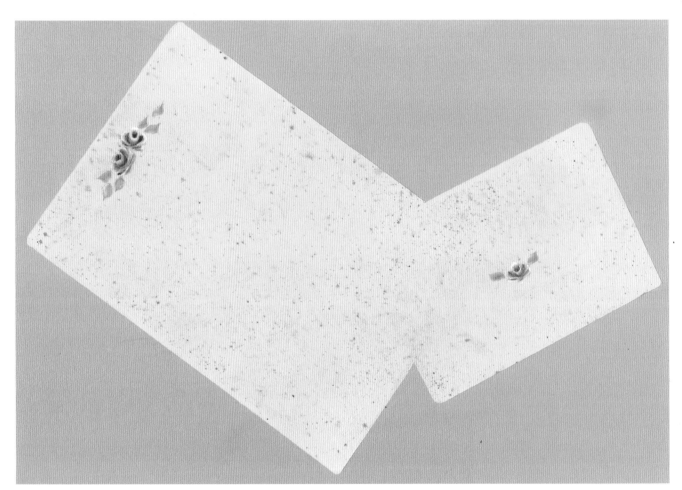

Here the roses and leaves are complete on the spattered stationery and envelope.

10 Leaves

Basecoat the leaves with a brush mix of the color below. Do not mix the colors thoroughly; this way, each leaf will have a slightly different look.

Leaves
Raw Sienna + Cadmium Yellow Mid + Unbleached Titanium + tad Paynes Grey + tech Burnt Umber

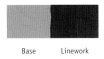

Base   Linework

11 Shadows on Stationery and Envelope

Please note that this particular design uses a light source that is above and slightly to the left, casting shadows to the front of the objects. The change of light source helps to maximize the effects of dimensions and realism for this particular design.

You are now ready to add the shading around the outside edges of the stationery and the fold lines on the envelope. Moisten the surface with Retarder and Antiquing Medium. Side load the ¼-inch (6mm) angular brush with the light shading mix. Shade around the envelope and paper, feathering out the shading more on the left side and bottom of each. Make the shading much smaller on the right side and top of each. Load the brush with the dark shading mix, and shade very close to the outside edge of the stationery and envelope. Place this shade over the light shading (see image on page 58).

Light Shade
Raw Sienna + Burnt Umber + Permanent Alizarine + tad Unbleached Titanium + tad Paynes Grey

Dark Shade
Light shade mix + more Burnt Umber

Base   Light shade   Dark shade

12 Liner

Use the liner color on a liner brush to paint veins and stems on the leaves, and accent lines around the roses on the stationery and envelope.

Liner
Burnt Umber + Permanent Alizarine + tad Unbleached Titanium

Value Blending and Refining

13 Pen

Basecoat the pen. Base the gold parts of the pen with solid coverage using the medium gold value. Detail the underside of the nib of the pen with Carbon Black on the liner brush. Let it dry.

Pen
Paynes Grey, Burnt Umber, Unbleached Titanium, Titanium White, Cadmium Yellow Mid, Carbon Black
- Base: PG + BU
- Light: UT
- Highlight: TW + CYM = Warm White
- Shade: Pen base mix + tad CB

Base   Shade   Hi Lt

Gold on Pen
Cadmium Yellow Mid, Raw Sienna, Permanent Alizarine, Burnt Umber, Titanium White
- Medium: CYM + RS
- Light: Medium mix + CYM + tad TW
- Highlight: CYM + tad TW
- Dark: Medium mix + BU + PA
- Low Dark: BU + PA

Hi Lt   Lt   Med   Dark   Lo Dk

End of Pen
- Base: Rose shade mix
- Highlight: UT
- Shade: BU

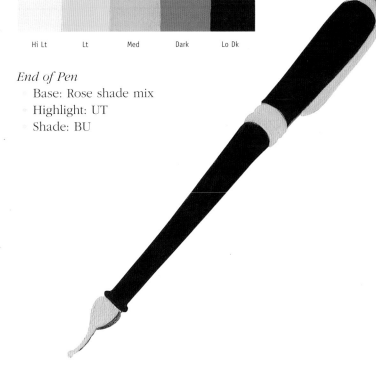

Pen Value Placement Map

oooo = Highlight
∴∵∴ = Light
M = Medium
/// = Dark
XXX = Low Dark

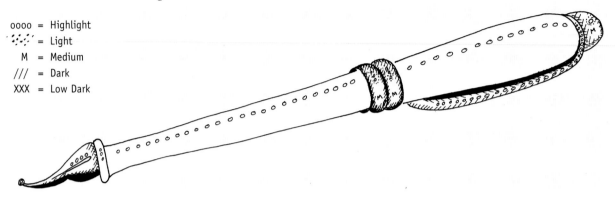

14 Basecoat the main part of the pen again. While the paint is still wet, add the light value, then the highlight and shading. For the gold part of the pen, add the light value, then highlight. Paint in the dark value, then the low dark. Add the remaining values to the end of the pen. Add retarder as needed.

Step 14 Add light and dark values to the pen.

15 Shade the pen and add more details to the nib with Carbon Black.

16 Dry the surface with a hair dryer. Allow it to cool to room temperature. Remove any graphite lines with odorless solvent. Remove any excess solvent with a dry paper towel. Seal the entire surface with Clear Glazing Medium.

Step 15 Complete the shading on the stationery and envelope and the values on the pen.

Highlights, Shading and Shadows

Refer to the glazing map for placement. All highlights, shines, shading, reflected light and cast shadows are applied to a surface that is moistened with Retarder and Antiquing Medium.

17 Stationery and Envelope

Highlight
1. Add a light shine to the left side of the stationery and the left side of the envelope flap using Unbleached Titanium.

Shading
1. Strengthen the shading around the outside edge of the stationery and the envelope using the dark shading mix.

Cast Shadow
1. Paint the cast shadow from the flap of the envelope onto the envelope with Burnt Umber.

18 Pen

Highlight
1. Titanium White + tech Cadmium Yellow Mid (= Warm White)
2. Add a stronger shine using Titanium White.

Reflected Light
1. Ultra Blue Deep + tad Titanium White + Iridescent Blue
2. Add a stronger shine using more Titanium White + Iridescent Blue.

Shading
1. Carbon Black

Glazing Map

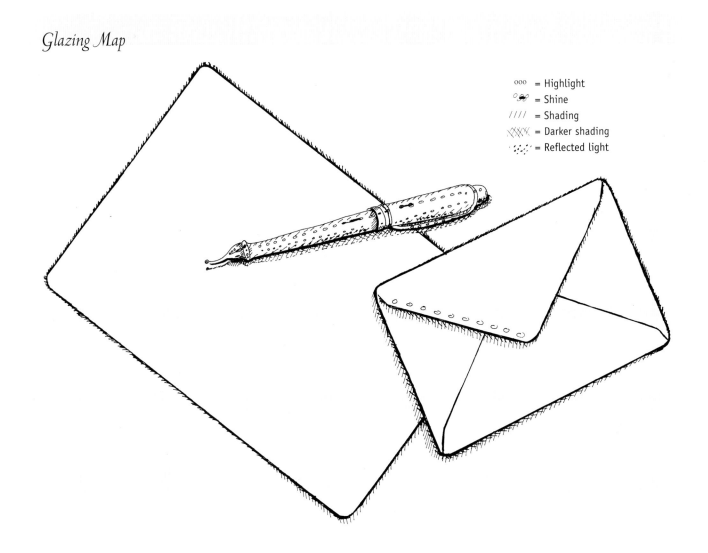

ooo = Highlight
᛫ = Shine
//// = Shading
XXXX = Darker shading
᛫᛫᛫ = Reflected light

19 Gold on Pen

Highlight
1. Highlight gold mix
2. Highlight gold mix + Titanium White

Shading
1. Burnt Umber

Reflected Light
1. Ultra Blue Deep + Titanium White

Cast Shadow
1. Carbon Black

Place a contact shadow where the outer edges of the stationery and envelope touch the table.

Because of the reflectiveness and roundness of the pen, there are two shines. The one on top is closest to the light source so paint it brighter.

Place a slight highlight on this raised edge of the envelope flap.

Place the cast shadow from the nib of the pen a short distance from the actual nib. This tells the viewer that the nib is raised off the surface of the stationery.

Remember that all cast shadows are darkest at the contact point.

Let the corner of the stationery protrude over the trim to enhance the trompe l'oeil effect.

Paint the cast shadow from the flap of the envelope longer on this side to show that the flap is slightly raised.

20 Painting the Trim

Using painter's tape, mask off a ¼-inch (0.6cm) margin around the outer edge of the box. Paint the trim with a mixture of Paynes Grey, Ultra Blue Deep, Carbon Black and a tad Cashmere. Be careful to paint around the lower left corner of the stationery. This enhances the trompe l'oeil effect.

Paint all the edges of the box in this same manner.

Trim mix

21 Finishing

Seal the surface with a coat of Clear Glazing Medium. Allow to dry and apply at least six coats of varnish.

Victorian Rose Teacup

To create the super realism needed for trompe l'oeil, certain techniques are used. One, called the invasion technique, is to paint some objects protruding out of the painting. Creating a niche or cabinet where the rear wall is pushed back is known as the evasion technique.

In this trompe l'oeil study, the evasion technique is used. The cup appears to be hanging in a small recessed cabinet that was created through a one-point perspective, giving the illusion of depth. The small confines give the feeling of intimacy within the painting. The hanging cup with its high contrasting shadows, the lace doily hanging over the front edge of the shelf and the cabinet with its illusion of depth set the stage for this dynamic piece.

Materials

Silver Brush Ltd. Brushes

no. 2 5020S Chisel Blender
no. 8 5020S Chisel Blender
no. 14 5020S Chisel Blender
⅛-inch (3mm) 5319S Wee Mop
¼-inch (6mm) 5319S Wee Mop
no. 8 5019S Refining Mop
⅛-inch (3mm) 5006S
    Blending Floating Angular
¼-inch (6mm) 5006S
    Blending Floating Angular
¾-inch (19mm) 5006S
    Blending Floating Angular
1-inch (25mm) 2008S Square Wash
1-inch (25mm) 2514S Wash
    for varnishing
no. 20/0 2422S Ultra Mini Script Liner
no. 1 2522S Monogram Liner
no. 2 1721S Stencil Mini

Jo Sonja's Chroma Acrylics

Titanium White (TW)
Raw Sienna (RS)
Cadmium Yellow Mid (CYM)
Cadmium Yellow Lt (CYL)
Ultra Blue Deep (UB)
Burnt Umber (BU)
Permanent Alizarine (PA)
Olive Green (OG)
Pthalo Green (PthG)
Carbon Black (CB)
Rich Gold (RG)

Background Colors

Damask Rose
Deep Plum

Jo Sonja's Mediums

All Purpose Sealer
Retarder and Antiquing Medium
Clear Glazing Medium
Flow Medium
Gloss varnish
Matte varnish

Additional Supplies

general materials listed in chapter one

Surface

from Custom Wood by Dallas

Background Preparation

1 Fill any nail holes or wood joints with Jo Sonja's Water Based Wood Filler. Allow this to dry for one hour, then sand to a refined finish. Wipe down and remove the dust with a lint-free cloth. Mix two parts Deep Plum with one part All Purpose Sealer (2:1). Then to seven parts of the paint and sealer mix, add one part Flow Medium (7:1). Mix well with a palette knife and apply with a 1-inch (25mm) wash brush to the wooden cabinet. When dry, wet sand the cabinet to a refined finish. Apply another coat, let dry and buff with a piece of brown paper bag.

2 Mix two parts Damask Rose and one part All Purpose Sealer (2:1). Then to seven parts of this paint and sealer mix, add one part Flow Medium (7:1). Mix well with a palette knife. Use this mix to paint the insert, applying two coats with a sponge roller to achieve an eggshell finish. Dry and sand between coats. Buff the final coat with a piece of brown paper bag. Trace the design, then prove the tracing of the cup, doily and cabinet. At this time, transfer only the cabinet lines onto the surface.

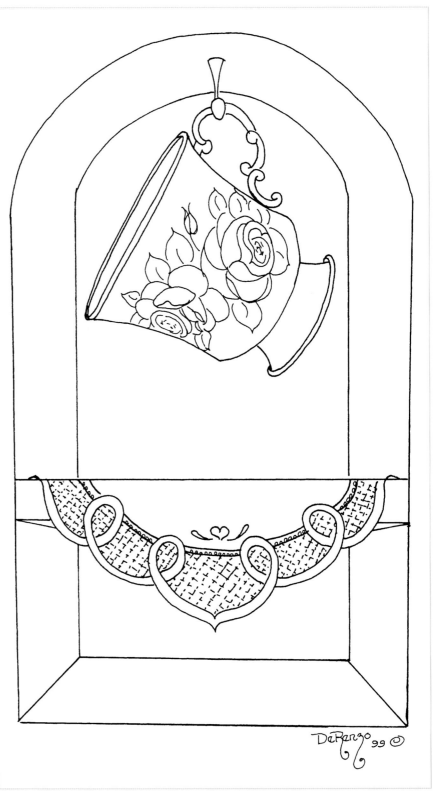

This pattern may be hand-traced or photocopied for personal use only. Enlarge at 111 percent to bring it to full size.

Value Blending and Refining

3 Background

Following the value placement map, base in the values for the background using the mixes below. Paint and refine the blending as well (as described in chapter four), then let dry completely.

Background

Damask Rose, Titanium White, Raw Sienna, Burnt Umber, Permanent Alizarine

- Warm Black: BU + UB = WB mix
- Light: Damask Rose + TW + RS
- Highlight: Light mix + TW + tad RS
- Medium: Damask Rose
- Dark: Damask Rose + BU + PA
- Low Dark: Dark mix + BU + tad PA

Note: tad = small amount; tech = less than a tad

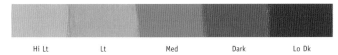

| Hi Lt | Lt | Med | Dark | Lo Dk |

Background Value Placement Map

Hi Lt = Highlight
Lt = Light
Med = Medium Light
Dk = Dark
xxxx or Lo Dk = Low Dark

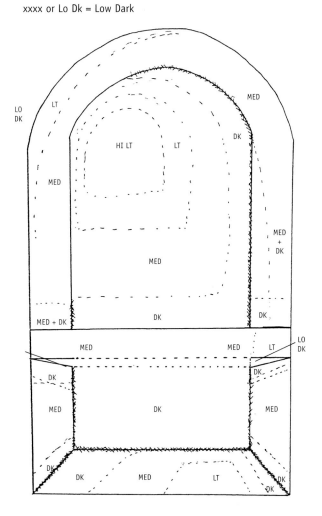

4 Teacup

Transfer the pattern for the teacup and cup hook onto the surface. Do not transfer the doily or the rose design onto the cup. Base in the values for the main part of the teacup. Basecoat the handle of the cup with the medium mix, then shade with the dark and low dark values.

Teacup
Titanium White, Burnt Umber, Ultra Blue Deep, Raw Sienna
- Medium: TW + WB mix + medium background mix + RS
- Light: Medium mix + TW + RS
- Highlight: Light mix + TW + tad RS
- Dark: Medium mix + WB mix + medium background mix
- Low Dark: Dark mix + WB mix

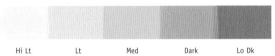

Hi Lt	Lt	Med	Dark	Lo Dk

5 Gold Trim and Cup Hook

Base in the values for the gold trim on the cup and the cup hook. Base in the gold trim on the handle with the medium gold mix, then shade with the high dark, dark and low dark gold mixes. Complete the refine blending on the entire cup and cup hook.

Gold Trim and Cup Hook
Cadmium Yellow Mid, Raw Sienna, Burnt Umber, Permanent Alizarine
- Medium: CYM + RS
- Light: Medium gold mix + CYM
- Highlight: CYM
- High Dark: Medium gold mix + RS + tech PA
- Dark: High dark gold mix + BU + tad PA
- Low Dark: Dark gold mix + BU

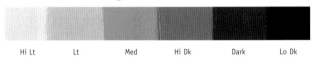

Hi Lt	Lt	Med	Hi Dk	Dark	Lo Dk

Teacup and Hook Value Placement Map

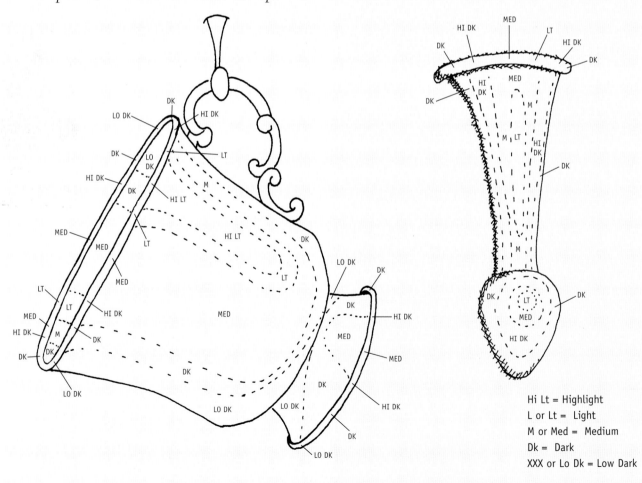

Hi Lt = Highlight
L or Lt = Light
M or Med = Medium
Dk = Dark
XXX or Lo Dk = Low Dark

6 Cabinet Glazes

Using the 1-inch (25mm) square wash brush, moisten the entire surface with Retarder and Antiquing Medium. Apply the glazes with values that are semitransparent to transparent. After each application, soften with a mop brush. Refer to the glazing map on page 71 for guidance.

Cabinet Glazes
Burnt Umber, Ultra Blue Deep, Permanent Alizarine, Carbon Black, Pthalo Green

- Warm Black: BU + UB = WB mix
1. Glaze Mix Medium: PA + WB mix
   This glaze mix gives the depth to the inside of the cabinet. Apply several applications to the area on the map marked for shading for the desired depth or darkness.
2. Glaze Mix Dark: WB mix
   This glaze is used for the lines that define the interior cabinet. This is not applied as liner work but as a glaze over a surface that is moistened with Retarder and Antiquing Medium. Apply this to the area on the map marked for darker shading.
3. Shadow Glaze: CB + PthG
   To make the shadow more exciting and to add a color vibration, the cabinet's complementary color is added to the shadow glaze. Pthalo Green is used because its pure intensity won't be overpowered by the Carbon Black. Apply this glaze to the cast shadow areas from the cup, tablecloth and arch inside the cabinet.

Med   Dark   Shadow

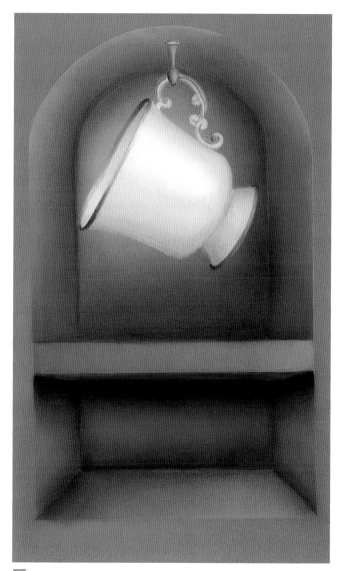

7
Dry the surface and remove any graphite lines with odorless solvent. Do any background touchup, let dry, and seal off the entire painting with Clear Glazing Medium. Let it dry completely.

8 Leaves

Transfer the roses and leaves onto the teacup. Because the roses and leaves are placed on the teacup, the teacup becomes the background color. To enable the roses and leaves to rest well against the teacup, some of the teacup mixes were added into the roses' and leaves' value mixes.

The base coat for the leaves will be semitransparent because of the use of retarder. Use the light mix where leaves fall on the highlight and light value areas of the teacup. Use the medium mix where leaves are placed on the medium value areas of the teacup, and the dark mix on the dark and low dark values areas of the teacup. When the leaves are dry, moisten the surface with Retarder and Antiquing Medium. Side load the ¼-inch (6mm) angular brush with the low dark leaf mix and add the center veins and shading on the leaves.

Leaves
Olive Green, Ultra Blue Deep, Permanent Alizarine, Titanium White, Cadmium Yellow Mid
- Medium: OG + light teacup mix
- Light: Medium leaf mix + highlight teacup mix
- Dark: OG + UB + medium teacup mix
- Low Dark: Dark teacup mix + UB + OG+ PA
- Tints: UB + TW

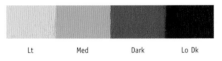

9 Roses

Basecoat the roses with the medium values, then let them dry. Moisten the area with Retarder and Antiquing Medium and add the highlight and light values. Then paint in the dark and low dark values in the appropriate areas for shading and petal separation. Place some dark red rose mix inside the bowl of the white rose. Refer to the photos and value placement map.

White Rose
Titanium White, Burnt Umber, Ultra Blue Deep, Raw Sienna
- Light: Light tablecloth mix + TW
- Medium: Medium tablecloth mix + tad TW
- Dark: Dark tablecloth mix
- Low Dark: Low dark tablecloth mix + BU + UB
- Tints: RS, TW + tech UB

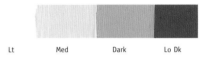

Red Rose
Permanent Alizarine, Olive Green, Burnt Umber
- Light: Medium white rose mix
- Highlight: Light white rose mix
- Medium: Light teacup mix + PA + OG
- Dark: Medium teacup mix + BU + PA
- Low Dark: Dark teacup mix + BU + PA

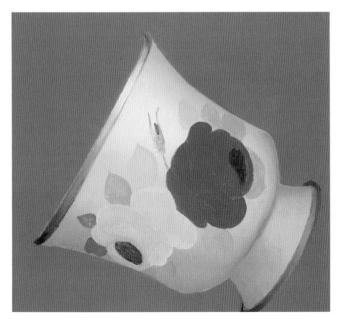

Basecoat the leaves and roses with the medium value mixes. The values of the leaves change from light to low dark as they move away from the light source. The center of the white rose is base-coated with the dark red rose value. The center of the red rose is based with the low dark red rose value.

10 Rouging

The rouging around the rose design on the teacup is Raw Sienna and Permanent Alizarine + Raw Sienna. When the surface is dry, moisten the teacup with Retarder and Antiquing Medium. Then side load the ½-inch (12mm) angular brush into the desired color. Blend the paint out on a waxed palette until it is transparent. Apply this transparent paint around the roses and leaves. Soften with a mop brush.

11 Sealing Teacup

When the rose design is dry, remove any graphite lines with odorless solvent. Do any necessary touchups and dry again. Seal the teacup with Clear Glazing Medium and let it dry completely.

12 Tablecloth

Transfer the pattern lines for the tablecloth onto the surface. The lacework is a series of tiny dashes. The heart and comma stitchwork is tiny horizontal lines. First place the low dark value on the left and pull tiny lines to the right. Then place the light value on the right and pull to the left, slightly overlapping the low dark lines. Shade the outer edge of the light area (commas and heart) with the low dark value.

Tablecloth
Raw Sienna
- Light: Light teacup mix + RS
- Medium: Medium teacup mix + RS
- Dark: Dark teacup mix + dark gold trim mix
- Low Dark: Low dark teacup mix + low dark gold trim mix
- Accents: RS, PA + WB mix

| Lt | Med | Dark | Lo Dk |

Rose Detail Value Placement Map

ooo = Light to highlight values
xxxx = Dark to low dark values

To finish all the highlights and shading, you will need to moisten with retarder several times. Allow the surface to dry before adding more retarder.

Tablecloth Value Placement Map

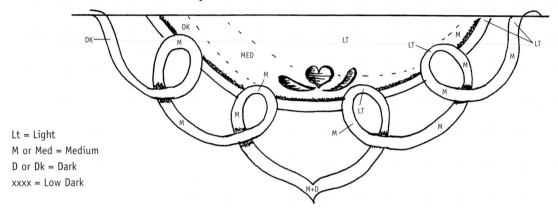

Lt = Light
M or Med = Medium
D or Dk = Dark
xxxx = Low Dark

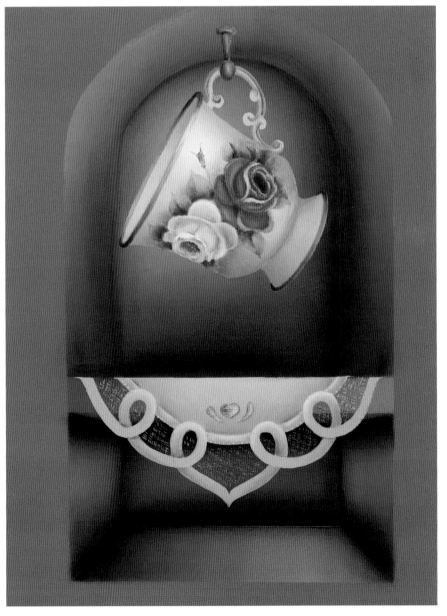

After adding rouge color around the leaves and flowers and completing the tablecloth, seal the surface with Clear Glazing Medium. You're now ready to begin the final highlights and shading.

Highlights, Shading and Shadows

Refer to the glazing map for placement. Moisten the surface with Retarder and Antiquing Medium before painting all the highlights, shines, shading, reflected lights and cast shadows.

13 Teacup

Highlight

1. Add a wide, transparent float of the highlight teacup mix. Soften with a mop. Remember to keep this value confined to the highlight value zone of the teacup and go right over the rose design. On the foot or pedestal of the cup, the first highlight is the medium teacup mix. On the back inside edge of the teacup use the light teacup mix.
2. Then add a flip-float of Titanium White + a tech of Cadmium Yellow Mid (= Warm White), and soften with a mop. The second highlight on the pedestal of the cup is the light teacup mix. This is as bright as you will make the pedestal.
3. Into the wet flip-float, add a final shine of Titanium White. Soften with a mop brush.

Shading

Apply the shading in very transparent layers.
1. Low dark teacup mix + Warm Black. Soften with a mop.
2. Warm Black. Several applications of the Warm Black shading may be required to achieve the desired depth. Soften after each application with a mop.

Reflected Light
1. Ultra Blue Deep + Titanium White
2. First mix + more Titanium White. Soften with a mop after each application.

14 Gold Trim and Cup Hook

Highlight

1. Float Cadmium Yellow Mid on the front rim of the teacup. Pull the color a little to the right and left and soften with a mop. Highlight the back rim of the teacup with the light gold trim mix. Highlight the handle and foot trim with the medium gold trim mix.
2. Next add Cadmium Yellow Lt to the front rim of the teacup, Cadmium Yellow Mid to the back rim of the teacup, and the light gold trim mix to the handle and foot trim of the teacup.
3. The final and brightest shine to the front rim of the teacup is Titanium White + a tad of Cadmium Yellow Lt.
4. Place the highlights on the cup hook in the following order: medium gold mix, then the light gold mix and finally Cadmium Yellow Mid.

Glazing Map

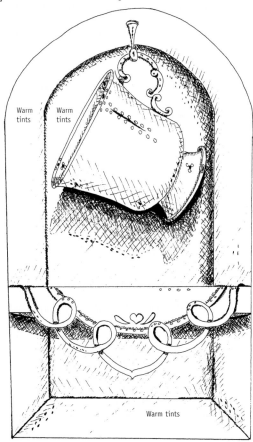

oooo = Highlights
°⚬⚬ = Shines
//// = Shading
xxxxx = Darker shading
⸫⸳⸫ = Reflected light
⸳⚬⸳ = Shine on reflected light

Warm tints

Warm tints

Warm tints

Shading

1. Low dark gold trim mix
2. Burnt Umber + Permanent Alizarine. This darker shading is applied as a very thin transparent line along the top and bottom of the rims, in the darkest curves of the gold trim on the handle and on the cup hook.

Reflected Light
1. Ultra Blue Deep + Titanium White
2. First mix + more Titanium White. Soften with a mop after each application.

Because light travels in a straight path, place a warm glaze here as well as in the lower right corner.

Give the highlight a slight curve so it follows the curvature of the cup. Place a lighter primary shine within the highlight.

Place a highlight shine on the inside back edge of the teacup. It should not be as bright as the primary shine.

Add just a hint of cool tint to the outside edge of the shadows to enhance the contrast of the shadows.

Allow a bit of the glazes to remain on the tablecloth.

Add a warm glaze to the front edge where the light would enter into the painting.

Add cool tints to the darker areas of the cabinet.

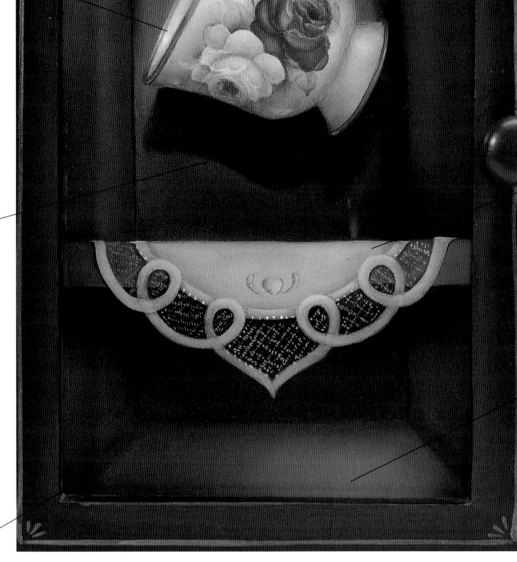

15 Tablecloth

Highlights
1. Highlight tablecloth mix + Warm Black
2. Highlight tablecloth mix + tech Titanium White + tech Raw Sienna

Shading
1. Low dark tablecloth mix
2. Shade under the tablecloth where the cloth touches the shelf with a very thin line of Warm Black + tad Permanent Alizarine.

16 Cabinet

Add more depth to the inside of the cabinet by adding in more of the Cabinet Glazing Mix. Soften with a mop. Allow a bit of this glaze to remain on the tablecloth.

17 Cast Shadows

Paint the cast shadows from the teacup and the cabinet with Carbon Black + Pthalo Green. Paint the shadows so they are semitransparent and have value change. The closer they are to the edge of the object that is casting the shadow, the darker they will be.

18 Cool Tints

Add cool tints and some reflected light of Ultra Blue Deep + tad Titanium White to the interior of the cabinet. Adding a cool tint along the outside edge of the teacup's cast shadow helps to emphasize and bring attention to the shadow, adding a subtle contrast.

19 Warm Tints

Add warm glazes of Raw Sienna + techs of Titanium White to the interior of the cabinet where the path of light would enter (the front lower shelf, the back upper left and upper left side).

20 Finishing

Let this dry for one to two weeks (or speed-dry with a hair dryer), then brush on one coat of Clear Glazing Medium. Dry overnight and varnish with a mixture of matte and gloss varnish. Apply at least three coats, drying between coats and buffing with Super Film.

   Seal the cabinet with one coat of Clear Glazing Medium. Allow it to dry. Antique the outside of the cabinet with a mixture of Permanent Alizarine + Warm Black. Basecoat the inside edge of the door with the low dark background mix. Bring some of the color onto the outside edge of the door. When the antiquing is dry, add the liner work using Rich Gold + tech Permanent Alizarine + tech Deep Plum. Dry and seal with Clear Glazing Medium. Let dry.

   Varnish the cabinet with a mixture of matte and gloss varnish. Apply three or more coats, drying between coats and buffing with Super Film. Secure the painted Masonite into the opening of the cabinet door.

Quilting
Guild
Monday
at
8 oo

The Collection Shelf

This project is not only a study of the invasion and evasion trompe l'oeil techniques, but it covers the four basic object shapes: sphere (pincushion), cube (tole tin box), cylinder (candles and spool of thread) and cone (candle snuffer). The design is a one-point perspective that incorporates all three points of view (bird's eye, worm's eye and eye level).

This is a low-key painting, meaning that the majority of values range from low light to black. Light values are used, but they are used sparingly and are usually kept in the focal area to establish the center of interest. This low-key painting is made more dynamic with the use of a complementary red and green color scheme and a close light source that creates dramatic shadows to give the viewer a sense of intimacy with the painting.

Materials

Silver Brush Ltd. Brushes
no. 2 5020S Chisel Blender
no. 4 5020S Chisel Blender
no. 8 5020S Chisel Blender
no. 16 5020S Chisel Blender
¼-inch (3mm) 5006S
   Blending Floating Angular
¼-inch (6mm) 5006S
   Blending Floating Angular
½-inch (12mm) 5006S
   Blending Floating Angular
¾-inch (19mm) 5006S
   Blending Floating Angular
no. 20/0 2422S Ultra Mini Script Liner
no. 10 5003S Blending Stroke Filbert
no. 8 5003S Blending Stroke Filbert
¼-inch (3mm) 5319S Wee Mop
¼-inch (6mm) 5319S Wee Mop
no. 8 5019S Refining Mop
1-inch (25mm) 2008S Square Wash
1-inch (25mm) 2514S Wash
   for varnishing
no. 12/0 2400S Ultra Mini
   Pointed Round
no. 20/0 2407S Ultra Mini Script Liner
no. 0 1721S Stencil Mini
no. 2 1721S Stencil Mini

Jo Sonja's Chroma Acrylics
Titanium White (TW)
Cadmium Yellow Mid (CYM)
Raw Sienna (RS)
Burnt Umber (BU)
Carbon Black (CB)
Napthol Crimson (NC)
Pthalo Blue (PthB)
Ultra Blue Deep (UB)
Paynes Grey (PG)
Background Color
Forest Green

Jo Sonja's Mediums
All Purpose Sealer
Retarder and Antiquing Medium
Clear Glazing Medium
Flow Medium
Gloss varnish
Matte varnish

Additional Supplies
general materials listed in chapter one

Surface
from Valhalla Designs

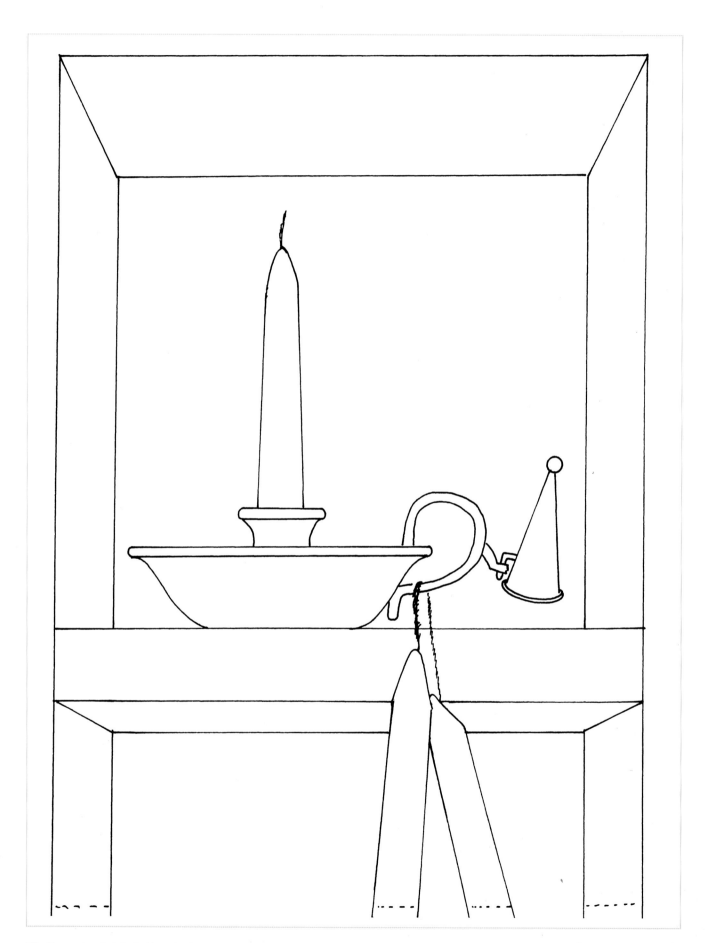

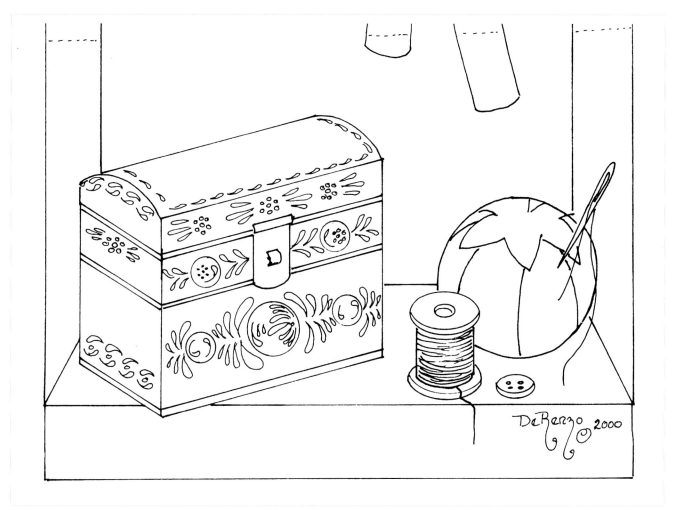

These patterns may be hand-traced or photocopied for personal use only. They appear here at full size. Connect the patterns at the dotted line.

Background Preparation

1 Fill any nail holes or wood joints with wood filler. Allow to dry, then sand to a refined finish. Wipe down and remove the dust with a lint-free cloth. Create a mixture of Napthol Crimson and Forest Green (1:1). To two parts of this mixture add one part All Purpose Sealer (2:1). Finally, to seven parts of the paint and sealer mix, add one part Flow Medium (7:1). Mix well with a palette knife and apply with a 1-inch (25mm) wash brush to the wooden frame. Apply at least two coats, wet sanding between coats.

2 Mix Forest Green + Cadmium Yellow Mid + Ultra Blue Deep + a tad of Titanium White. To two parts of this mixture, add one part All Purpose Sealer (2:1). To seven parts of the paint and sealer mixture, add one part Flow Medium (7:1). Mix well with a palette knife. Use this mix to paint the inset, applying two coats with a sponge roller to achieve an eggshell finish. Dry and sand between coats. Buff the final coat with a piece of brown paper bag. Trace and prove the design. Transfer just the shelf and cabinet inset using a transparent graph ruler to ensure straight lines.

Value Blending and Refining

3 Background for Shelf and Inset

As with the Victorian Rose Teacup project, the background for this piece is also part of the painting and the illusion of the niche and shelf must be painted first. Tape off each section of the shelf with painter's masking tape for easier painting. Use the value placement map for reference.

Background for Shelf and Inset
Forest Green, Cadmium Yellow Mid, Ultra Blue Deep, Titanium White, Carbon Black, Pthalo Blue

- Medium: FG + CYM + UB + TW
- Light: Medium mix + CYM + TW + tech UB
- Highlight: Light mix + CYM + TW + tech UB
- Dark: Medium mix + CB + UB + PthB + tech CYM
- Low Dark: Dark mix + CB + UB + PthB + tech CYM

Note: tad = small amount; tech = less than a tad

Hi Lt	Lt	Med	Dark	Lo Dk

Background Value Placement Map

Hi Lt = Highlight
Lt = Light
Med = Medium
Dk = Dark
Lo Dk or //// = Low Dark

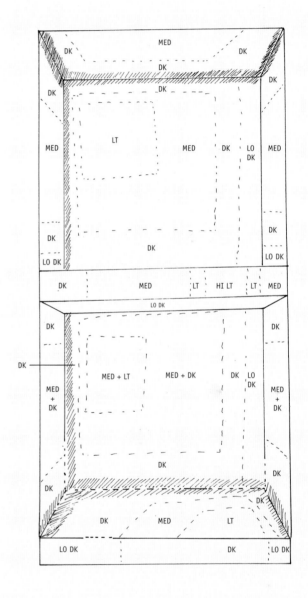

4 Allow the background refine blending to dry, then seal the surface with one coat of Clear Glazing Medium. When the glazing is dry, transfer the pattern for the candleholder, candles, pincushion and tole tin box onto the surface. Do not transfer any of the decoration on the tin box at this time.

5 Pincushion and Red Candles

Form is always first, so paint the pincushion values like a sphere (see illustrations on page 80). The red hue I used for the pincushion and candles is Napthol Crimson. I chose to tone this pure red with its complement, Forest Green, which is also the main background color. I also used Forest Green as the mother color for most of the other mixes.

Pincushion and Red Candles
Napthol Crimson, Forest Green, Cadmium Yellow Mid, Titanium White, Carbon Black, Raw Sienna
- Medium: NC + FG
- Light: Medium mix + NC + CYM + tech TW
- Highlight: Light mix + CYM + tech TW
- Dark: Medium mix + FG (if mix becomes too muddy, add a bit of NC)
- Low Dark: Dark mix + NC + FG + CB

Hi Lt   Lt   Med   Dk   Lo Dk

Step 3 Blend and refine the values of the background.

6 When the pincushion sphere is dry, transfer the section lines onto the pincushion. Reactivate the paint with retarder and blend each section separately, referring to the value placement map. Let this dry, then transfer the pattern for the green top, wooden spool and thread, button and needle. See steps 10 and 11 for completing the spool and thread.

7 Pincushion Top
To help the pincushion come forward in the painting, the green mixes for the top are much warmer than the background color.

Pincushion Top
- Highlight: Background mix + RS + highlight red pincushion mix + tech TW
- Light: Background mix + RS + light red pincushion mix
- Medium: Background mix + RS + medium red pincushion mix
- Dark: Background mix + RS + dark red pincushion mix
- Low Dark: Background mix + RS + low dark red pincushion mix

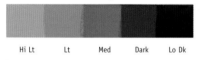

Hi Lt   Lt   Med   Dark   Lo Dk

Sphere Value Placement Map

Hi Lt = Highlight
Lt = Light
Med = Medium
Dk = Dark
Lo Dk or /// = Low Dark

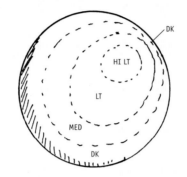

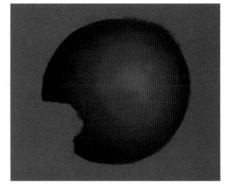

Blended and refined values for the pincushion.

Pincushion Value Map

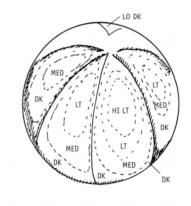

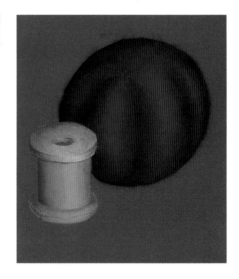

Pincushion Top Value Placement Map

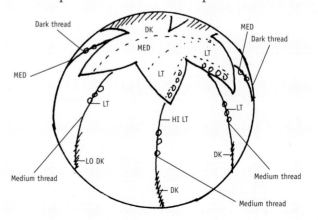

8 Tole-painted Tin Box

For easier painting, place painter's tape around the outer edges of the box. When painting the lid, think of it as a cylinder lying on its side.

Tole-painted Tin Box
Carbon Black, Forest Green, Paynes Grey, Titanium White, Raw Sienna

- Medium: CB + FG + PG + tech TW
- Light: Medium mix + tad TW + tad RS
- Highlight: Light mix + tad TW + tad RS
- Dark: Medium mix + PG + FG + CB
- Low Dark: Dark mix + CB + PG

| Hi Lt | Lt | Med | Dark | Lo Dk |

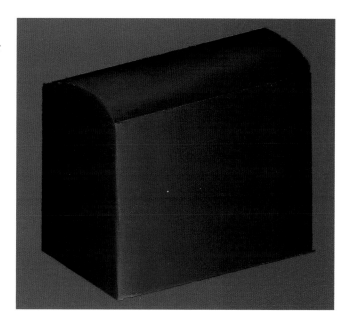

9 Button and Band on Box

Once the box is dry, transfer the pattern for the banding onto the surface. Place painter's tape along each edge for easier painting. The values for the banding need to be in alignment with the values on the box. Note that although the mixes below begin with the candleholder mixes, they end up being much warmer after the addition of Raw Sienna. (See illustrations of banding on page 82.)

Button and White Band on Box
Raw Sienna, Titanium White, Napthol Crimson

- Highlight: Highlight candleholder mix + RS + TW
- Light: Light candleholder mix + RS
- Medium: Medium candleholder mix + RS + TW
- Dark: Dark candleholder mix
- Low Dark: Low dark candleholder mix
- Accent on Button: NC + RS

| Hi Lt | Med | Dark |

Tin Box Value Placement Map

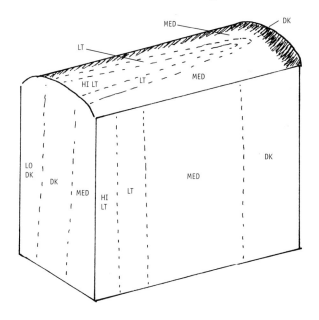

Button Value Placement Map

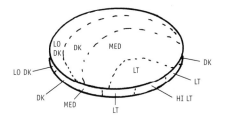

Band on Box Value Placement Map

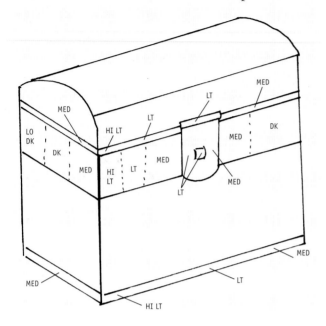

The values on the band should align with the values on the box. See page 81 for a picture of the box with values blended and refined.

10 Blue Thread and Blue Candle

Paint the blue thread as a cylinder. The thread lines will be added in the decoration stage.

Blue Thread and Blue Candle
Ultra Blue Deep, Cadmium Yellow Mid, Napthol Crimson, Titanium White, Carbon Black, Pthalo Blue

- Medium: UB + Orange (CYM + NC) + TW + tech medium green background mix
- Light: Medium mix + TW + tech CYM + tech light green background mix
- Highlight: Light mix + TW + tech highlight green background mix
- Dark: Medium mix + UB + tad dark green background mix
- Low Dark: Dark mix + UB + CB + low dark green background mix + tech PthB

| Hi Lt | Lt | Med | Dark | Lo Dk |

Thread and Spool Value Placement Map

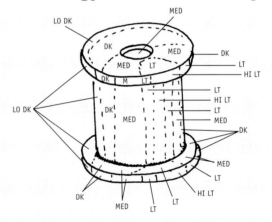

Hi Lt = Highlight
Lt = Light
Med = Medium
Dk = Dark
Lo Dk = Low Dark

11 Wooden Spool

Basecoat and refine the values for the wooden part of the spool.

Wooden Spool
Raw Sienna, Burnt Umber, Titanium White, Cadmium Yellow Mid
- Medium: RS + BU + TW + medium green background mix
- Light: Medium mix + TW + RS + light green background mix
- Highlight: Light mix + TW + tech CYM + tech highlight green background mix
- Dark: Medium mix + BU + tad medium red pincushion mix + dark green background mix
- Low Dark: Dark mix + tad low dark red pincushion mix + tad low dark green background mix

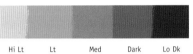

Hi Lt   Lt   Med   Dark   Lo Dk

Candle, Candleholder and Candle Snuffer Value Placement Map

Hi Lt = Highlight
Lt = Light
M or Med = Medium
Dk = Dark
Lo Dk or //// = Low Dark

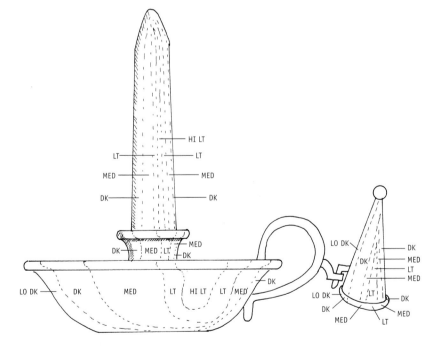

12 Candleholder, Candle Snuffer and Needle

Basecoat the handle of the candleholder with the medium value, shade with the low dark and highlight with the medium value, then with the light value.

Basecoat the top of the candle snuffer with the medium value, highlight with the light value, and shade with the low dark.

Basecoat the needle with medium value using a liner. Highlight with the highlight value; shade with the low dark Value. Note that all the mixes are very close in value.

Candleholder and Needle
Titanium White, Raw Sienna, Carbon Black, Burnt Umber, Napthol Crimson
- Medium: TW + RS + CB + medium green background mix
- Light: Medium mix + TW + RS
- Highlight: Light mix + CB + BU + medium green background mix
- Dark: Medium mix + CB + BU + medium green background mix
- Low Dark: Dark mix + BU + CB + low dark green background mix
- Turning Color: NC

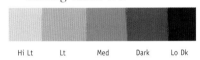

Hi Lt   Lt   Med   Dark   Lo Dk

13
Dry the surface with a hair dryer. Allow it to cool to room temperature. Remove any graphite lines with odorless solvent, then remove any excess solvent with a dry paper towel. Seal the entire surface with Clear Glazing Medium. When dry, transfer the pattern for the decoration onto the tin box.

Decoration

14 Decoration on Tin Box

Use the no. 12/0 pointed round to pull these tiny strokes and the no. 20/0 script liner for any fine lines.

Tin Box
- All Red Design: Medium red pincushion mix
- All Gray Design: Medium button mix
- All Gold Design: Raw Sienna
- All Green Design: Light green top mix
- All Black Design: Low dark tin box mix

15 Thread

At the outer edges, pull fine lines into the medium value area using the low dark blue thread mix. Make sure that you slightly curve these lines to follow the contour of the cylinder shape. In the highlight area, pull tiny lines into the medium value area using the blue thread highlight mix. Use the no. 20/0 script liner for these decorations.

16 Candlewicks

First, line the candlewicks with Carbon Black. Add tiny thread lines using the medium candleholder mix, then highlight with the highlight candleholder mix.

17 Sealing

When all the decoration is dry, again seal the tole-painted tin box with Clear Glazing Medium. Allow it to dry.

Highlights, Shading and Shadows

Refer to the glazing map on page 86 for placement. Apply all highlights (except for any drybrushing), shines, shading, reflected light and cast shadows to a surface that is moistened with Retarder and Antiquing Medium. Any time retarder is used, soften the paint with an appropriate-sized mop brush.

18 Shelf and Inset

Highlight
1. Using the highlight shelf mix, strengthen the highlight areas.
2. Strengthen again using the highlight shelf mix + Titanium White + tech Cadmium Yellow Mid.

Shading
1. Strengthen the shading inside the cabinet using the low dark shelf mix.
2. Strengthen again, especially the separation areas, using the low dark shelf mix + Carbon Black.

Reflected Light
1. Ultra Blue Deep + Titanium White

19 Pincushion

Highlight
1. Using the no. 0 stencil mini, drybrush the highlight pincushion mix in the highlight value areas, the light pincushion mix in the light value areas and the medium pincushion mix in the medium value areas. This is as light and bright as the pincushion will get because the pincushion is behind the button and thread and it is not made of a reflective material.

Shading
1. Low dark pincushion mix + Carbon Black

Reflected Light
1. Ultra Blue Deep + tad Titanium White
2. Add stronger shine using Titanium White + Ultra Blue Deep.

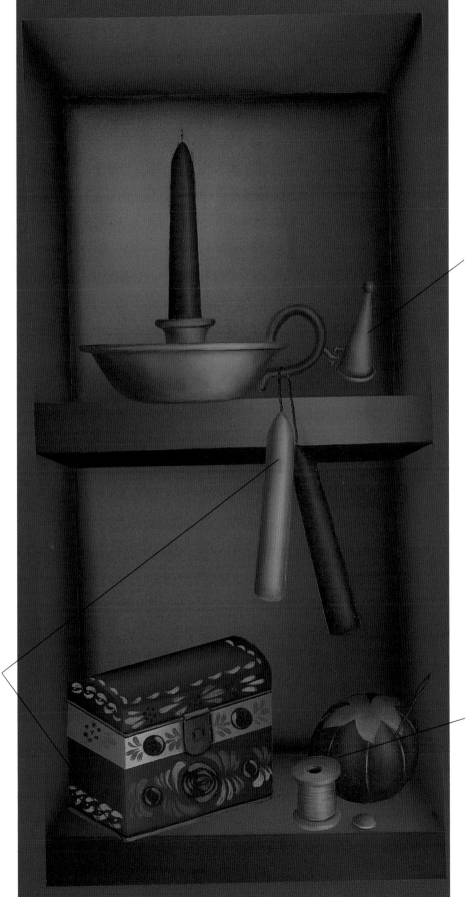

Even though this portion of the design is at eye level, the turned position of the candlesnuffer helps to create depth.

The invasion technique is accomplished by placing the candles and the corner of the box in front of the shelves. This doesn't appear to be realistic until the cast shadows are added.

The evasion technique is accomplished by placing the pincushion, thread and button away from the edge and inside the niche. Again, this becomes more realistic once the cast shadows are added, especially the cast shadow from the pincushion onto the back wall of the niche.

Glazing Map

oooo = Highlight
o-o-o-o = Shine
///// = Shading
XXXXX = Darker shading
XXXXX = Reflected light

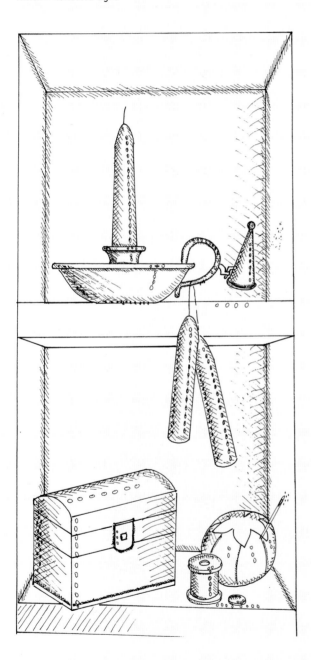

20 Red Candle

To ensure that the candle stays a bright red and to keep it from becoming muddy, place a wash (transparent application) of retarder + Napthol Crimson over the candle before adding any highlights or shading.

Highlight
1. Highlight pincushion mix
2. Highlight pincushion mix + tad Titanium White
3. Titanium White + tech Cadmium Yellow Mid + tech highlight pincushion mix

Shading
1. Low dark pincushion mix + Carbon Black

Reflected Light
1. Ultra Blue Deep + Titanium White
2. Titanium White + Ultra Blue Deep

21 Pincushion Top

Highlight
1. Highlight green top mix
2. Highlight green top mix + tech Titanium White + tech Cadmium Yellow Mid. Place this highlight on the front-most separating threads.

Shading
1. Low dark green top mix + Carbon Black
2. Strengthen it again, especially the separation areas, using the low dark green top mix + Carbon Black.

22 Tin Box

Highlight
1. Highlight tin box mix. Skip over the light gray banding with this mix.
2. Highlight tin box mix + Titanium White. Go over the entire front edge including the light gray banding.

Shading
1. Carbon Black. Paint this on in semitransparent to transparent washes. You will probably need two applications to achieve the desired depth.

Reflected Light
1. Ultra Blue Deep + tad Titanium White
2. Add a stronger shine using Titanium White + Ultra Blue Deep.

23 Blue Thread and Blue Candle

Highlight
1. Highlight blue thread mix. On the thread, place this highlight right on top of the thread lines.
2. Highlight blue thread mix + tad Titanium White + the smallest tech of Cadmium Yellow Mid.
3. Titanium White + tech Cadmium Yellow Mid + tech highlight blue thread mix. This is the final shine on the candle only.

Shading
1. Low dark blue thread mix + Carbon Black + tech Pthalo Blue

Reflected Light
1. Ultra Blue Deep + Titanium White
2. Titanium White + Ultra Blue Deep

24 Wooden Spool

Highlight
1. Highlight wooden spool mix
2. Highlight wooden spool mix + tad Titanium White + tech Cadmium Yellow Mid

Shading
1. Low dark wooden spool mix + tad Titanium White + tech Cadmium Yellow Mid
2. Burnt Umber + tad Carbon Black. Use this mix to make the tiny groove lines to the front edge.

25 Candleholder

Highlight
Remember, drybrushing requires a dry surface, so paint the rims after all of the drybrushing is completed.
1. Drybrush the front cup portion of the candleholder using the highlight candleholder mix. On the holder portion that is actually holding the candle, drybrush with the light candleholder mix. On the rims, apply retarder to the surface and apply the highlight candleholder mix to the front rim, light candleholder mix to the rim that is holding the candle and medium candleholder mix to the handle. On the candle snuffer apply retarder and flip-float on the medium candleholder mix. Use this mix on the rim of the candle snuffer as well.
2. Drybrush the highlight candleholder mix + tad Titanium White + tech Cadmium Yellow Mid onto the front cup portion of the candleholder. On the portion that is holding the candle, use the highlight candleholder mix. Apply retarder to the rims, then paint the front rim with the highlight candleholder mix + Titanium White + tad Cadmium Yellow Mid. Highlight the back rim with the highlight candleholder mix. Apply the light candleholder mix to the

handle. Apply retarder to the candle snuffer and flip-float on the light candleholder mix; add this to the candle snuffer rim as well.
3. Apply retarder to the surface. Paint a flip-float shine onto the cup portion of the candleholder using Titanium White + tech Cadmium Yellow Mid (Warm White). Apply this Warm White mix to the front rim. To the portion that holds the candle, add a flip-float of highlight candleholder mix + tad Titanium White + tech Cadmium Yellow Mid. Apply this to the rim as well.
4. Add a final shine into the wet flip-float on the front cup portion and rim with the Warm White mix. To the portion that holds the cup and its rim, highlight with the highlight candleholder mix + tad Titanium White + tech Cadmium Yellow Mid. To the candle snuffer and its rim, add a final shine using the light candleholder mix.

Shading
1. Low dark candleholder mix + Carbon Black
2. Carbon Black

Reflected Light
1. Ultra Blue Deep + Titanium White
2. Titanium White + Ultra Blue Deep

26 Needle

Highlight
1. Titanium White + tech Cadmium Yellow Mid (Warm White)

Shading
1. Carbon Black

27 Button

Highlight
1. Highlight button mix
2. Highlight button mix + tad Titanium White + tech Cadmium Yellow Mid

Shading
1. Low dark button mix + Carbon Black
2. The holes in the button are Carbon Black.

28 Cast Shadows

Paint the cast shadows with Carbon Black + a tad of Napthol Crimson applied semitransparent to transparent. Pay special attention to the detail of the contact shadows. This includes the red candle sitting in the holder, the wick on the handle of the candleholder, the needle inserted into the pincushion, the green top and threads on the pincushion and the blue thread where it touches the wooden spool and the shelf.

The upper right-hand light source casts a lower left shadow. When the shadow is cast onto the side wall of the niche, it becomes slightly rounded.

Place the reflected light slightly below the shelf line. This pulls the candleholder out in front of the shelf.

It is easier to put the cast shadow from the shelf onto the back surface before painting the candles. Remember, the shadow must also follow the rules of perspective.

After the values are painted for the spool of thread, add the individual threads, then the highlights and cast shadows.

No light reaches this corner, so it is almost pure black. Placing the cool tint next to the cast shadow enhances the dramatic effect.

29 Finishing

Antique the frame using a highlight glaze of Napthol Crimson. Place this on the inside edge close to the painting and cork opening, fading out as it gets closer to the outside edge.

Seal the surface with a coat of Clear Glazing Medium. Allow it to dry and apply at least six coats of varnish.

Cast Shadow Map

New Life

I n this high-key, complementary still life, we will be focusing on several different techniques for developing textures. Even when painting texture, the most important focus is still developing the form of an object. Two different specialty brushes will be introduced in this project to help create some of these textures. My special thanks to my friend Debbie Cole for introducing me to her Cole Scruffy brush.

Materials

Silver Brush Ltd. Brushes
no. 2 5020S Chisel Blender
no. 4 5020S Chisel Blender
no. 6 5020S Chisel Blender
no. 12 5020S Chisel Blender
no. 16 5020S Chisel Blender
⅛-inch (3mm) 5006S Blending
   Floating Angular
¼-inch (6mm) 5006S
   Blending Floating Angular
½-inch (12mm) 5006S
   Blending Floating Angular
¾-inch (19mm) 5006S
   Blending Floating Angular
no. 0 2101S Cole Scruffy
⅛-inch (3mm) 5319S Wee Mop
¼-inch (6mm) 5319S Wee Mop
no. 8 5019S Refining Mop
no. 16 5518S Mop
no. 0 1721S Stencil Mini
no. 2 1721S Stencil Mini
no. 6 5003S Blending Stroke Filbert
no. 8 5003S Blending Stroke Filbert
¼-inch (6mm) 2528S
   Filbert Grass Comb
no. 0 2522S Monogram Liner
1-inch (25mm) 2008S Square Wash
1-inch (25mm) 2514S Wash
   for varnishing

Jo Sonja's Chroma Acrylics
Titanium White (TW)
Cadmium Yellow Mid (CYM)
Indian Yellow (IY)
Naples Yellow Hue (NY)
Napthol Red Lt (NRL)
Cadmium Orange (CO)
Ultra Blue Deep (UB)
Permanent Alizarine (PA)
Paynes Grey (PG)
Burnt Umber (BU)
Burnt Sienna (BS)
Raw Sienna (RS)
Carbon Black (CB)
Background Color
Sky Blue

Jo Sonja's Mediums
All Purpose Sealer
Retarder and Antiquing Medium
Clear Glazing Medium
Flow Medium
Pickling White Wood Stain Glaze
Gloss varnish
Matte varnish

Additional Supplies
general materials listed in chapter one
old toothbrush

Surface
from Smooth Cut Wood

This pattern may be hand-traced or
photocopied for personal use only.
Enlarge at 120 percent to bring it to
full size.

Background Preparation

1 Fill any nail holes or wood joints with wood filler. Allow to dry, then sand to a refined finish. Wipe down and remove any dust with a lint-free cloth. Mix equal parts Titanium White + Ultra Blue Deep + Cadmium Yellow Mid for a mix I'll refer to as Robin's Egg Blue. To two parts of Robin's Egg Blue, add one part All Purpose Sealer (2:1).

Finally, to seven parts of the paint and sealer mix, add one part Flow Medium (7:1); I'll refer to this mix as the medium background mix. Mix well with a palette knife. Apply two coats to the inset with a sponge roller to achieve an eggshell finish. Dry and sand between coats.

Value Blending and Refining

2 Mix the values below. Moisten the entire surface with a generous amount of Retarder and Antiquing Medium. Using the 1-inch (25mm) square wash brush, start with the highlight mix and apply it to the surface. Then side load the brush into the light mix and start blending it out. Keep working the values side by side, blending next into the medium mix, then the dark, and finally the low dark. If the paint starts to dry or get tacky, tap your brush into the Retarder and Antiquing Medium to help loosen the paint and continue to blend. You should have a smooth gradation of values from the highlight mix to the low dark mix. Refer to the background value placement map and chapter four on backgrounds.

Blended Background
Titanium White, Cadmium Yellow Mid, Burnt Umber, Payne's Grey
- Medium: Background mix
- Light: Medium mix + TW + tad CYM
- Highlight: Light mix + TW + tech CYM
- Dark: Medium mix + BU + PG
- Low Dark: Dark mix + BU + PG

Note: tad = small amount; tech = less than a tad

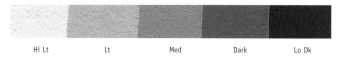

| Hi Lt | Lt | Med | Dark | Lo Dk |

Background Value Placement Map

Lt = Light
Med = Medium
Dk = Dark
Lo Dk = Low Dark

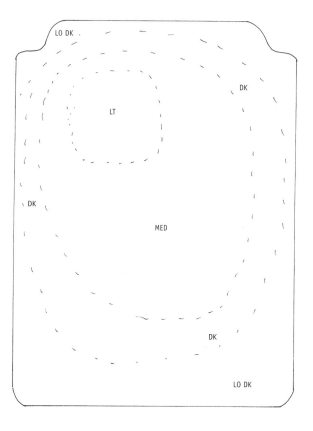

3 Allow the surface to dry thoroughly and buff to a smooth finish with a piece of brown paper bag. Apply one coat of Clear Glazing Medium and allow it to dry again. Trace and prove the design before transferring it onto the surface.

4 Watering Can

Tape off sections of the watering can (the body, top, handle and spout) as you paint them. At this time, blend the watering can, ignoring the ridges that encircle it. Refine the blending as well.

Watering Can
Titanium White, Raw Sienna, Burnt Umber, Paynes Grey, Napthol Red Lt

- Medium: TW + RS + PG + BU (This mix should lean slightly toward the blue side.)
- Light: Medium mix + TW + tad RS
- Highlight: Light mix + TW + tad RS
- Dark: Medium mix + PG + BU
- Low Dark: Dark mix + PG + BU
- Turning Color: NRL + RS

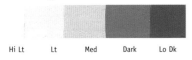

Hi Lt · Lt · Med · Dark · Lo Dk

Watering Can Value Placement Map

Hi Lt = Highlight
Lt = Light
M or Med = Medium
Dk = Dark
Lo Dk = Low Dark

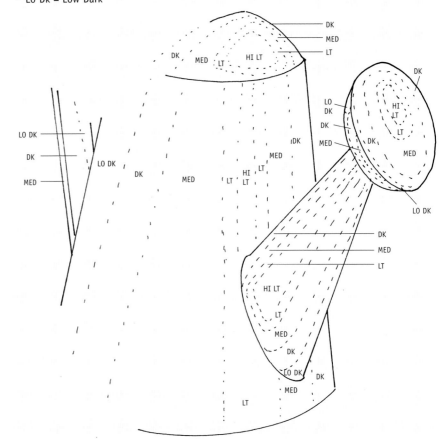

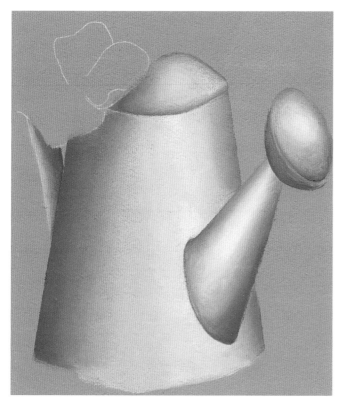

Step 4 Base in values on watering can.

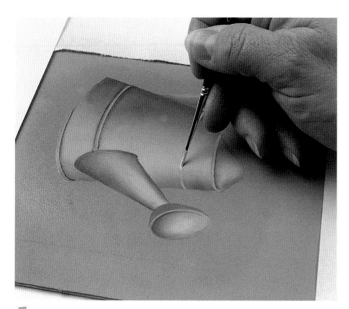

5 Place the ridges on using a liner and the medium to light mixes. Shade with dark to low dark on each side of the ridges. Add the highlight mix in the appropriate areas. Turning the surface sideways helps to keep the curvature of the ridges in proper alignment.

6 Rust Marks

Moisten the surface with retarder. Place one color at a time, lightly softening with a mop after each application. The colors are placed in this order: Raw Sienna, Burnt Sienna, Burnt Umber and Warm Black (Burnt Umber + Paynes Grey). The colors should softly blend into each other, with the Raw Sienna covering the most space and Warm Black covering a small area in the center.

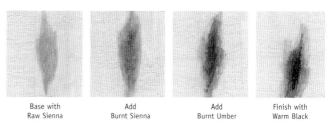

Base with Raw Sienna | Add Burnt Sienna | Add Burnt Umber | Finish with Warm Black

7 Front Poppies

It might take a bit of imagination, but form must be taken into consideration when painting flowers. Most of the poppies in this design fall into the category of an open cylinder, with minor modifications being made to create ruffles on the individual petals.

Front Poppies
Cadmium Orange, Indian Yellow, Titanium White, Naples Yellow Hue, Napthol Red Lt, Burnt Sienna, Paynes Grey

- Medium: CO + medium background mix
- Low Light: IY + tad medium mix + light background mix
- Light: IY + tech low light mix + TW + tech highlight background mix
- Highlight: NY + tech highlight background mix + tech TW
- Dark: NRL + tad medium mix + BS
- Low Dark: NRL + BS + tad PG

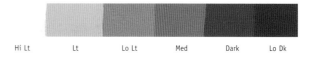

Hi Lt | Lt | Lo Lt | Med | Dark | Lo Dk

Poppies Value Placement Map

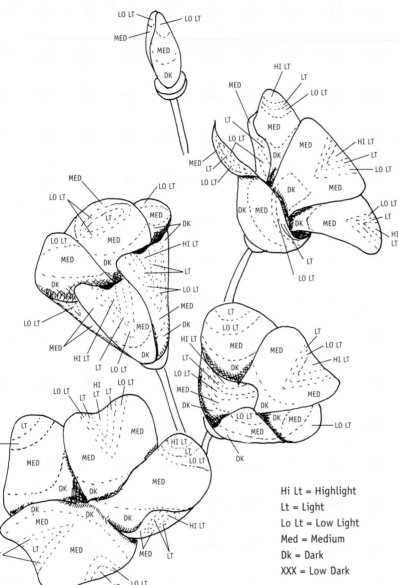

When basing in the values, remember that the first stage always looks choppy. At this stage, getting solid coverage and value change is more important than achieving a smooth look.

Hi Lt = Highlight
Lt = Light
Lo Lt = Low Light
Med = Medium
Dk = Dark
XXX = Low Dark

8 Rear Poppies

The rear poppies are toned and subdued more than the front poppies, focusing the viewer's attention to the front poppies where the light source would first touch this flower arrangement. This is accomplished by adding some of the background value mixes into the poppy value mixes. This not only tones the mixes because it is a mother color, but it also neutralizes the orange because blue is its complement.

Rear Poppies

- Highlight: Highlight front poppy mix + tad more highlight background mix
- Light: Light front poppy mix + light background mix
- Medium: Medium front poppy mix + medium background mix
- Dark: Dark front poppy mix + dark background mix
- Low Dark: Low dark front poppy mix + low dark background mix

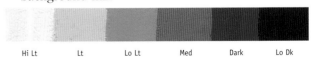

| Hi Lt | Lt | Lo Lt | Med | Dark | Lo Dk |

9 Flower Center

Using a liner, pull little strokes toward the center of the poppy using the low light mix. Shade at the bottom using the dark mix. Highlight toward the top using the light mix. Using the dark greenery mix, fill in the center, pulling a little bit of this green into the orange strokes. Add tiny dots in the center using the light greenery mix. See step 10 for greenery mixes.

10 Greenery

Basecoat in all of the greenery with the base mix below using a liner. Allow to dry. Moisten the surface with Retarder and Antiquing Medium and basecoat one sprig at a time with the base mix. While the paint is still wet, add the dark, low dark and light mixes. Again, as with everything else, the greenery must have form. The form for this particular greenery is a cylinder, so keep that in mind while painting. The light value is placed slightly to the right of the center. The dark values are on either side of each sprig, and the low dark value is on the left side only.

Greenery
Indian Yellow, Paynes Grey, Burnt Umber, Titanium White
  Base: Medium background mix + IY
  Light: IY + tech TW + tech base greenery mix
  Dark: Medium background mix + PG + BU + IY
  Low Dark: Dark background mix + PG + BU + IY

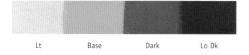

Lt	Base	Dark	Lo Dk

11 Bird's Nest

The nest falls into the category of an open cylinder lying on its side. The first step is underpainting the nest to help create its density. Moisten the surface with Retarder and Antiquing Medium using the no. 12 chisel blender, and quickly blend the values together, keeping them semitransparent (see page 98). Allow the surface to dry.

Bird's Nest
Raw Sienna, Burnt Sienna, Burnt Umber, Paynes Grey
  Light: RS
  Medium: BS
  Dark: BU
  Low Dark: BU + PG

Lt	Med	Dark	Lo Dk

Step 10 Paint in the values on the greenery.

Here the greenery is based in and the poppy has been refine-blended. Later, the glazing will give the flowers more dimension and life.

Nest Value Placement Map

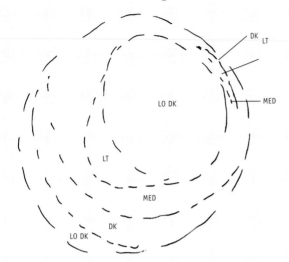

Step 11 Basecoat the values on the bird's nest.

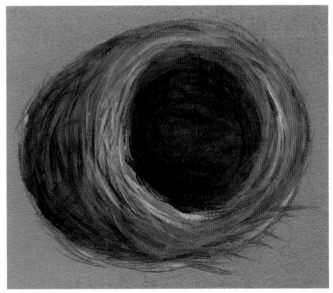

12 Moisten the surface with Retarder and Antiquing Medium. Line in the twigs in an uneven fashion by turning the painting surface and skipping around the nest. Start at the rear of the nest and work forward toward the light value. Keep the values of the twigs in line with the values of the nest. Pull a few of the twigs out beyond the outer edges of the nest to keep it from appearing too smooth. The inside of the nest should be kept quite dark with not too much detail at this time.

13 Use the liner brush to create the actual textures of the twigs and tendrils woven within the nest. The nest will have a more realistic appearance if you aim for variety in your liner detail, such as broken ends, change of direction and shape and a few hard angles. Use all of the values throughout the entire nest, but position the majority of the dark values toward the rear of the nest and the lighter ones toward the front. To actually create depth within the intertwined branches, paint the medium and light value twigs over darker twigs. Also, having value change on some of the individual twigs helps them appear to bend and intertwine within the nest. To accomplish this, paint the twigs so they are lighter as they come forward toward the light source and darker as they recede.

14 Robin's Eggs

Base in the values and refine blend. Let dry. Make a copy of the design and cut out just the eggs, exposing the eggs and covering the rest of the design. Very lightly moisten the eggs with Retarder and Antiquing Medium. Place the cutout over the eggs. Using an old toothbrush and Paynes Grey, spatter the eggs. Soften the dots by pouncing up and down lightly with a ¼-inch (6mm) Wee Mop.

Robin's Eggs
Ultra Blue Deep, Cadmium Orange, Titanium White, Raw Sienna, Cadmium Yellow Mid, Paynes Grey, Carbon Black, Napthol Red Lt
- Medium: UB + CO + TW
- Light: Medium mix + TW + tech RS
- Highlight: Light mix + TW + tech CYM
- Dark: Medium mix + UB + PG
- Low Dark: Dark mix + UB + PG + tech CB
- Turning Color: NRL

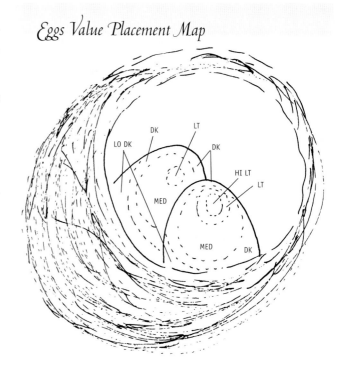

Eggs Value Placement Map

| Hi Lt | Lt | Med | Dark | Lo Dk |

15 Feather

Moisten the surface with Retarder and Antiquing Medium. Load a filbert grass comb brush with a mix of Burnt Umber and the dark watering can mix. Hold the brush vertical to the surface and, starting from the quill or center spine, pull out slightly, curving strokes that follow the direction of growth. Straighten the strokes as they come forward toward the tip of the feather. This first application appears very simplistic, but it gives shape to the feather.

16 Next, repeat the same process using just Burnt Umber. Add a few darker hairs with Burnt Umber + Paynes Grey. Lighten the tip of the feather using the highlight watering can mix. If the hairs of the feather appear too heavy, go back with the background color and paint some of the hairs out. Allow the surface to dry.

17 For the quill portion of the feather, moisten the surface with Retarder and Antiquing Medium. Starting at the tip of the feather, pull a line of Carbon Black, stopping where the feather hairs first begin. Clean out the brush and load it with the highlight watering can mix. Starting at the opposite, rounded end of the quill, pull this highlight mix toward the Carbon Black, continuing to pull a highlight down the center of the Carbon Black. Using Paynes Grey + Burnt Umber, shade on each side of the highlight area where the quill is wider and rounded. Using this same mix, pull out a few wispy hairs at the end of the quill with the liner.

18 Butterfly

Basecoat the butterfly with the following mixes.

Butterfly

- Top Wings: Basecoat in solid using a mix of the dark watering can mix + Naples Yellow Hue + tech Titanium White.
- Bottom Wings: Basecoat in solid Naples Yellow Hue + low light rear poppy mix
- Body: Basecoat in solid using a mix of the dark watering can mix + Burnt Umber (same as the first mix for the feather).

Top wings   Bottom wings   Top stippling   Bottom stippling   Light markings

19 After observing numerous photos of butterflies, I concluded that the wings were very textured, consisting of several tiny dots. In trying to recreate this effect, I decided to incorporate a wet-on-wet "stipple blending" technique. Moisten the surface with Retarder and Antiquing Medium, and basecoat the top and bottom wings again with their original base coat mix. While the base coat is still wet, moisten the Cole Scruffy into a small amount of retarder, and dip just the ends of the bristles into the appropriate paint mix. Lightly pounce the brush up and down onto a waxed palette until little dots of paint appear. Apply this textured shading onto the wet butterfly wings.

Top Wings Stippling

Dark watering can mix + Burnt Umber (same as the butterfly body mix). Then add a bit of Paynes Grey + Burnt Umber to this mix and stipple again, keeping it closer to the butterfly's body. Carry some of this darker mix onto the body.

Bottom Wings Stippling

Use the low light rear poppy mix along the top portion of the wing, and the dark watering can mix + Burnt Umber next to the body.

20 Fill in the light markings on the top wing using a mix of the highlight watering can mix + light rear poppy mix. Using a liner, create more texture by making tiny dots around the lighter markings and adding a design to the lower wing. First use a mix of Burnt Umber + tech of Paynes Grey, then a darker mix by adding more Paynes Grey to the Burnt Umber.

21 Add the final details of the vein lines running through the wings, legs and antennae with a mix of Paynes Grey + Burnt Umber.

22 Remove any graphite lines with odorless solvent. Allow to dry and seal the entire surface with one coat of Clear Glazing Medium.

Step 18 Basecoat the wings.

Step 19 Add texture to the wings with stippling.

Step 20 Tap in the dark markings.

Step 21 Add final details.

Glazing

A glaze is a transparent to semitransparent color that is applied over a dried opaque color. Glazing is used to make a color richer or add tints, accents, turning colors, reflected colors, reflected light and shadows. Glazing can also correct a color's temperature, intensity or value, and can add excitement to a painting with complementary vibration. In essence, it is what makes a good painting outstanding. Glazing is also the method I use for painting glass and water drops.

23 Watering Can

Any time you want to paint an object white, such as with the watering can, your first impulse might be to start out with a tube of pure white. But in painting the teacups in projects one and three, we learned that a white object is really painted in values of gray, which is how we basecoated the values for this watering can.

I would like the white for this watering can to appear quite warm. Adding very small amounts of Raw Sienna or Cadmium Yellow Mid to gray will warm the color quite nicely. But how do you make a gray appear even warmer without tinting it toward the green side? By putting a glaze of Raw Sienna over the entire watering can, I am able to achieve the desired warmth without turning my grays to green.

Application of Glazing
Moisten the entire surface with Retarder and Antiquing Medium. Pick up a small amount of Raw Sienna (or whichever glaze you're working with) and place it on your waxed palette. Add a little Retarder and Antiquing Medium and mix it well into the paint until you have a transparent wash of color. Apply this transparent wash (glaze) over the entire watering can (or whichever object you are glazing). Lightly soften any brush marks with the no. 8 refining mop. If the glaze gets painted onto an undesired area, remove it with a clean brush moistened with water.

24 Poppies

Warm the front two poppies with a glaze of Cadmium Yellow Mid. Glaze the back two poppies and the bud with light + medium background mix to tone and set them back in the painting.

25 Nest

Add a glaze of the light front poppy mix to the light area of the nest and the low light front poppy mix to the medium area of the nest. This color coordination helps to unify the painting.

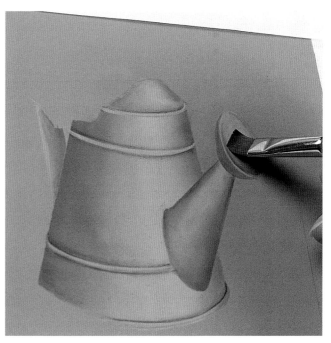

Step 23 Paint a glaze over the can to warm the color.

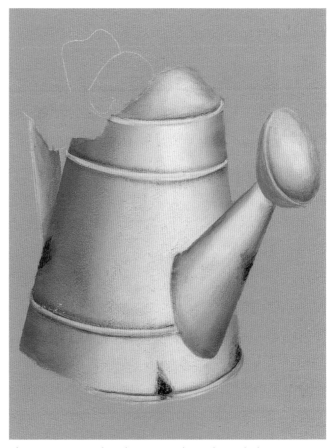

This watering can has the rust marks and initial glazing.

26 Butterfly

I wanted the butterfly to color coordinate with the painting, so I used colors that were already in my palette to paint it. Though this butterfly really does exist in nature, I took artistic license to tone and mute the colors, enabling it to enhance the painting without drawing too much attention away from the center of interest. Further tone the butterfly by glazing over it with a wash of the medium background mix.

27 Sealing

Once the glazing is finished, dry the surface and seal it with one coat of Clear Glazing Medium. Let this dry.

Highlights, Shading and Shadows

Refer to the glazing map for placement. Apply all highlights, shines, shading, reflected color, reflected light, glazes and cast shadows to a surface that is moistened with Retarder and Antiquing medium. Any time retarder is used, use appropriate-sized mops to soften the paint. Apply drybrushing highlights to a dry surface

28 Watering Can

Highlight
1. Drybrush using the highlight watering can mix. Bring this drybrushing right over the front of the ridges.
2. Drybrush again using the highlight watering can mix + Titanium White + tech Raw Sienna.
3. Moisten the surface with Retarder and Antiquing Medium and add a flip-float using Raw Sienna + Titanium White (= Warm White).
4. Add a final shine using Titanium White.

Shading
1. Strengthen the shading using the low dark watering can mix + Paynes Grey + Burnt Umber.
2. Strengthen again using transparent glazes of Paynes Grey + Burnt Umber (= Warm Black). This might take several applications. Be sure to strengthen the shading on each side of the ridges. Paint small dots for the holes on the spout with the bristle tip of a liner loaded with the Warm Black mix.

Reflected Light
1. Ultra Blue Deep + Titanium White
2. Titanium White + Ultra Blue Deep

Reflected Color
1. Medium front poppy mix

29 Poppy

Highlight
1. Moisten the surface with Retarder and Antiquing Medium. Strengthen the lights and highlights using the light poppy mix in the light areas and the highlight poppy mix in the highlight areas. Start with the rear mixes for the rear poppies and the front mixes for the front poppies.
2. Strengthen again using the highlight poppy mix in the light areas and the highlight poppy mix + tad Titanium White in the highlight areas.

Shading
1. Low dark front poppy mix + tech Carbon Black + tad Permanent Alizarine
2. Permanent Alizarine + Carbon Black. Make this mix very transparent and use sparingly.

Reflected Lights and Cool Tints
1. Ultra Blue Deep + Titanium White

Glazing Map

Raw Sienna glaze

○○○○	= Highlight
○○◎◎	= Shine
/////	= Shading
✕✕✕✕	= Darker shading
∴∴∴	= Reflected light
◎◎◎	= Reflected color

Raw Sienna glaze

Raw Sienna + Titanium White glaze

30 Greenery

Highlight
1. Strengthen the highlights using Indian Yellow + tech Titanium White.

Shading
1. Reinforce the shading using the low dark greenery mix + tad Paynes Grey + tad Cadmium Yellow Mid.

31 Robin's Eggs

Highlight
1. Highlight using the highlight robin's egg mix.
2. Highlight again using the highlight robin's egg mix + tad Titanium White + tech Cadmium Yellow Mid.

Shading
1. Reinforce the shading using the low dark robin's egg mix + Paynes Grey.
2. Reinforce again using Paynes Grey.

32 Bird's Nest

Highlight
1. Using a liner, add highlights with Raw Sienna + Titanium White + tech Cadmium Yellow Mid.
2. Add more highlights using the light and highlight front poppy mixes. Pull a few twigs over the front of the eggs.

Shading
1. Using a liner, reinforce the shading with the low dark bird's nest mix + Carbon Black.
2. Add a few more twigs with Carbon Black.

Reflected Light
1. With a liner, add some twigs using Ultra Blue Deep + Titanium White. Add a few lines of this reflected light to the inside of the nest.

33 Feather

Highlight
1. With a liner, add a few highlight hairs to the tip of the feather and to the middle front portion using the highlight watering can mix.
2. Highlight the light portion of the quill using the highlight watering can mix + Titanium White.

Shading
1. Add a few hairs of Carbon Black.

34 Butterfly

Shading
1. Separate the top front wing from the top back wing with a transparent shading of Paynes Grey + Burnt Umber (= Warm Black).

Water Drops

The illusion of a water drop seems to add a finishing touch of realism to your painting. When understood and created in a step-by-step systematic order, water drops are really quite easy to paint.

   Remember that water drops are fluid and are subject to the law of gravity. They are either in the process of being pulled toward a flat surface or are already resting on a level surface. Those being pulled (or falling) will be in the shape of a teardrop. Those on a flat surface will be oval in shape and flat on the bottom. The size of the water drop needs to be in proportion to the flower petal or leaf onto which it is placed.

Water Drops
- Background: Color of the object on which you place the drop + one value darker. For example, if your drop is placed in a medium value area, such as on the medium poppy petal or the medium value area of the watering can, you will color that area one value darker in the shape of the drop.
- Warm White: Titanium White + tech of Cadmium Yellow Mid
- Gray: Carbon Black + Titanium White. Mix this either one value lighter on a dark background or one to two values darker on a light background.
- Shadow: The value of the surface on which the water drop is resting + two values darker.

Teardrop Water Drop

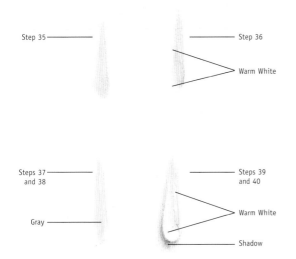

Step 35

Step 36

Warm White

Steps 37 and 38

Steps 39 and 40

Gray

Warm White

Shadow

Flat Water Drop

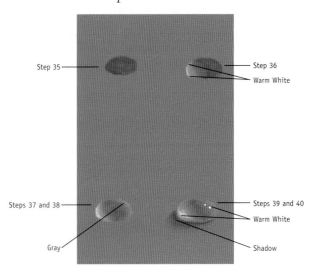

Step 35

Step 36

Warm White

Steps 37 and 38

Steps 39 and 40

Warm White

Gray

Shadow

35 Water Drop Procedure

Glaze the area with Retarder and Antiquing Medium where you wish to place your drop. Concentrate on one drop at a time as the area must remain wet. Place the water drop background color in the shape of the drop with the ⅛-inch (3mm) angular brush. Clean the brush with Retarder and Antiquing Medium and blot it on a paper towel.

36
Load one corner of the ⅛-inch (3mm) angular brush with Warm White, and blend on your waxed palette. Touch your brush down at seven o'clock. Gently work the paint up toward the top of the drop as well as toward the bottom, gently fading out toward the center. Clean the brush with Retarder and Antiquing Medium and blot it on a paper towel.

37
Load the ⅛-inch (3mm) angular brush with Gray. Touch down the brush at one o'clock. Gently fade the color toward the Warm White at the bottom right. If the drop is flat, fade the Gray toward the Warm White on the upper left (see illustration at top right). *Do not connect the gray and white areas* on the right bottom or left top of flat oval drops, or on top of falling drops. This will add to the illusion that the water drop is so transparent you can see right through it. Clean the brush in Retarder and Antiquing Medium and blot it on a paper towel.

38
Using a clean brush with a small amount of Retarder and Antiquing Medium in it, softly blend in the shape of your drop. If you have lost your dark value background, add some more, as it is essential to the illusion of transparency on the drop.

39
Reinforce the light area of Warm White at seven o'clock. Add two dots or a dot-dash of slightly thinned Warm White in the middle of the Gray upper right, but not exactly on the edge.

40
Remoisten the area if necessary with Retarder and Antiquing Medium. Load the corner of the ⅛-inch (3mm) angular brush with the water drop shadow color. Blend out on your waxed palette. Touch your brush on the outside edge of the drop at seven o'clock. Pull the color to the right and fade it out at about 5:30. Touch the brush with shadow color again at seven o'clock and pull the color up to the top while gently fading out. If the drop is flat, the shadow should follow the contour of the flat surface. If the drop is falling, the shadow should fall accordingly. If you need to reinforce the shadow area, let it dry and repeat this step.

These back poppies are cooler and more subdued than the front poppies.

Add some of the poppy's reflected color onto the water drop.

Equalizing the values on this edge of the spout with the value of the background gives the illusion that the spout recedes and curves back.

Keep the cast shadows from the spout and poppy petals very soft.

Add highlights to the front of the twigs where they are closer to the light source.

Add a few highlight hairs coming out from the quill.

DeRenzo
2000

41 Cast Shadows

Paint the cast shadows from opaque to semi-transparent and then transparent. The mix for the cast shadows from the bird's nest is Carbon Black + tad Permanent Alizarine. Carbon Black is used for the contact shadow of the watering can onto the surface, the twig that projects onto the surface and the feather. All of the cast shadows that fall onto the watering can are Paynes Grey + Burnt Umber (= Warm Black).

42 Foreground

To help lead the viewer's eye into the painting, add a warm glaze to the foreground in front of the feather, because this is where light would first enter. Moisten the surface with Retarder and Antiquing Medium. First add a glaze of the medium background mix, then the light background mix and finally Raw Sienna + tech Titanium White. Soften each application with a mop. Since light travels in a straight path, add a glaze of Raw Sienna to the light background above and around the back poppies.

43 Finishing

Seal the entire cabinet with a coat of Clear Glazing Medium. Allow this to dry and then lightly sand. Add retarder to Pickling White Wood Stain Glaze to increase working time, and apply it to the cabinet with the 1-inch (25mm) square wash brush. While the stain is still wet, streak in some of the dark background mix. When the surface is dry, moisten it again with retarder and put on a glaze of Raw Sienna. Let this dry again. Moisten the surface with retarder and antique the outer edges using the low dark background mix, then spatter with the same mix. Paint the edges and trim using the low dark background mix.

44 Dry and apply another coat of Clear Glazing Medium. Dry again and apply at least six coats of varnish.

December

Sun	Mon	Tue	Wed	Thu	Fri	Sat
						1
2	3	4	5	6	7	8
9	10	11	12	13	14	15
16	17	18	19	20	21	22
23	24	25	26	27	28	29
30	31					

Patti DeRenzo CDA

Let Your Light Shine

I almost never paint from a model, but because this particular design stretched me beyond my basic knowledge of light sources and reflections, I found it necessary to actually set up a sample in a window at night. I needed to see what would happen when the light source was a single lit candle reflecting in a window and where it would cast the shadows. I also needed to see what shadows were cast by the flame as an overhead light source.

I discovered that as the candle burned down, the shadows and location of the highlights constantly changed. This educated and challenged me immensely. Also, when the candle was lit, it became translucent at the top and dark in the center near the bottom. My hope as a teacher and artist is to share this knowledge with you.

Materials

Silver Brush Ltd. Brushes
no. 2 5020S Chisel Blender
no. 4 5020S Chisel Blender
no. 8 5020S Chisel Blender
no. 10 5020S Chisel Blender
no. 16 5020S Chisel Blender
⅛-inch (3mm) 5006S
    Blending Floating Angular
¼-inch (6mm) 5006S
    Blending Floating Angular
½-inch (12mm) 5006S
    Blending Floating Angular
¾-inch (19mm) 5006S
    Blending Floating Angular
no. 20/0 2422S Ultra Mini Script Liner
⅛-inch (3mm) 5319S Wee Mop
¼-inch (6mm) 5319S Wee Mop
¾-inch (19mm) 2008S Square Wash
1-inch (25mm) 2514S Wash
    for varnishing
no. 8 5019S Refining Mop
no. 20/0 2404S Ultra Mini Fan

Jo Sonja's Chroma Acrylics
Titanium White (TW)
Cadmium Yellow Mid (CYM)
Raw Sienna (RS)
Brown Earth (BE)
Napthol Red Lt (NRL)
Permanent Alizarine (PA)
Ultra Blue Deep (UB)
Paynes Grey (PG)
Burnt Umber (BU)
Carbon Black (CB)

Jo Sonja's Mediums
All Purpose Sealer
Retarder and Antiquing Medium
Clear Glazing Medium
Flow Medium
Gloss varnish
Matte varnish

Additional Supplies
general materials listed in chapter one

Surface
from Valhalla Designs

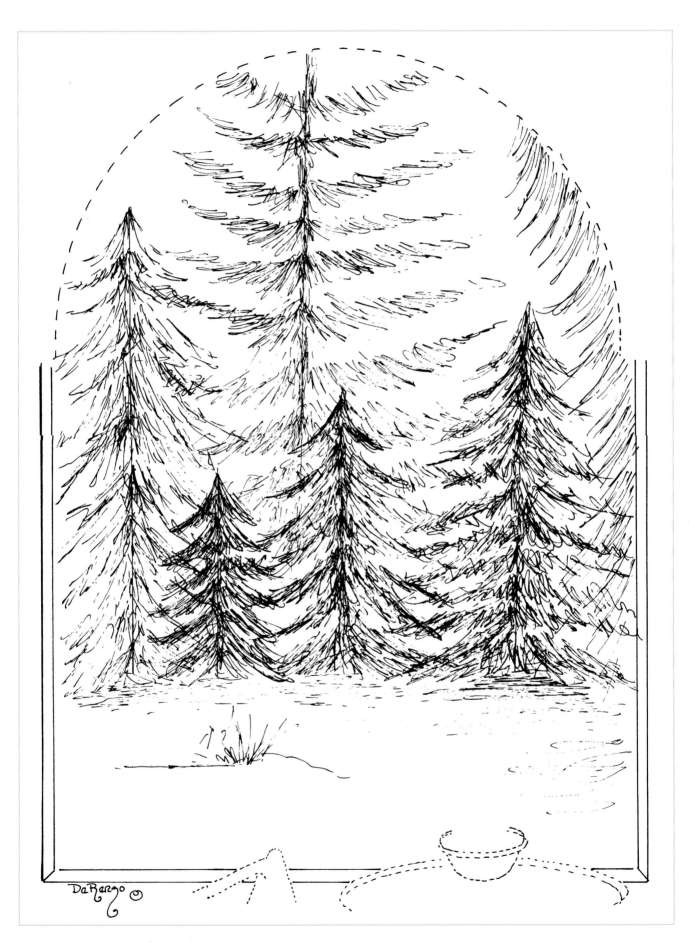

These patterns may be hand-traced or photocopied for personal use only. Enlarge the pattern at left at 111 percent to bring it to full size. Enlarge the above pattern at 154 percent to bring it to full size. Transfer the patterns separately, using the dashed lines at the bottom of the landscape portion to align them.

Background Preparation

1 Fill any nail holes or wood joints with wood filler. Allow to dry, then sand to a refined finish. Wipe down and remove any dust with a lint-free cloth. Mix Raw Sienna + Brown Earth + Titanium White for a mix I'll refer to as Medium Golden Tan. Mix two parts of Medium Golden Tan with one part All Purpose Sealer (2:1). Finally mix seven parts paint and sealer mix with one part Flow Medium (7:1). Mix well with a palette knife and apply to the wooden frame with the ¾-inch (19mm) square wash brush. Apply at least two coats, wet sanding between coats.

2 Mix Titanium White + Ultra Blue Deep + a tad of Permanent Alizarine for a color similar to periwinkle blue. To two parts of the paint mix, add one part All Purpose Sealer (2:1). Finally, to seven parts of the paint and sealer mix, add one part Flow Medium (7:1) for a mix I'll refer to as the medium background mix. Mix well with a palette knife. Apply two coats to the inset with a sponge roller to achieve an eggshell finish. Dry and sand between coats. Buff the final coat with a piece of brown paper bag. Trace and prove the design. Transfer on just the window ledges and window frame at this time.

Value Blending and Refining

3 Background

Tape off the inner edge of the window ledge and frame so that the landscape portion of the design can be painted first. Moisten the surface with Retarder and Antiquing Medium. Apply a generous amount of paint, starting with the dark value at the top. Next, add the medium and light values. Blend them softly into each other. Stop about halfway down the surface and clean out your brush with water. Load the brush into the low dark value and start at the bottom, working your way up. Next add the dark value. Stop where the dark and light values meet. Clean out the brush. Load it with retarder, then softly blend where the light and dark values meet.

Background
Ultra Blue Deep, Titanium White, Carbon Black, Permanent Alizarine, Paynes Grey
- Medium: UB + TW + tad PA
- Light: Medium mix + TW
- Dark: Medium mix + UB + CB + tad PA
- Low Dark: PG + CB

Note: tad = small amount; tech = less than a tad

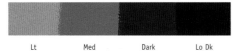

| Lt | Med | Dark | Lo Dk |

The lightest value is placed in the middle so it appears as though the moon has just come up over the horizon.

Background Value Placement Map

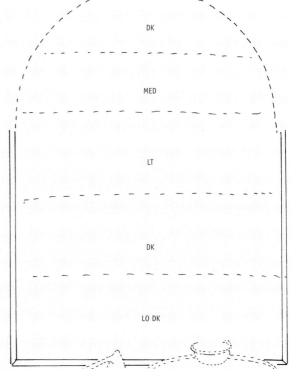

4 Trees

Base in the trunks of the trees using the low dark background mix for the back trees and Carbon Black for the front trees. With the no. 20/0 fan brush, paint the branches of the trees in a crisscross fashion, using the same color as was used for the trunks.

Add some snow to the front trees on top of the Carbon Black, using the medium background mix then the light background mix. With the medium background mix, use an angular brush to add a few snow mounds and a liner brush to add a few sprigs of grass. Shade behind the snow mounds with Carbon Black. Remove the tape.

5 Window Ledge and Frame

Mask off each area with tape and paint one section at a time, referring to the value placement map on page 114.

Window Ledge and Frame
Raw Sienna, Titanium White, Cadmium Yellow Mid, Brown Earth, Carbon Black
- Medium: RS
- Light: Medium mix + TW + tad CYM
- Highlight: Light mix + TW
- Dark: Medium mix + BE
- Low Dark: BE + CB

| Hi Lt | Lt | Med | Dark | Lo Dk |

6

Allow this to dry, then transfer the design for the candleholder and snuffer, candle, flame and matchsticks. Sand down any hard paint edge that runs through any part of the design. Do not transfer on the reflection at this time.

Step 4 Paint the tree branches with the fan brush.

The trees in the background are lighter and less dense. The foreground trees are painted more densely and darker, so the snow will be more visible.

7 Candleholder and Snuffer

In addition to the values on the map, paint the handle of the snuffer with the medium value, shade with the low dark value and highlight with the highlight value.

Candleholder and Snuffer
Carbon Black, Titanium White, Ultra Blue Deep, Raw Sienna, Napthol Red Lt
- Medium: CB + TW + UB + RS
- Light: Medium mix + TW + RS
- Highlight: Light mix + TW + RS
- Dark: Medium mix + RS + UB + CB
- Low Dark: Dark mix + UB + CB
- Accent and Turning Colors: NRL, RS

| Hi Lt | Lt | Med | Dark | Lo Dk |

Window Ledge and Frame Value Placement Map

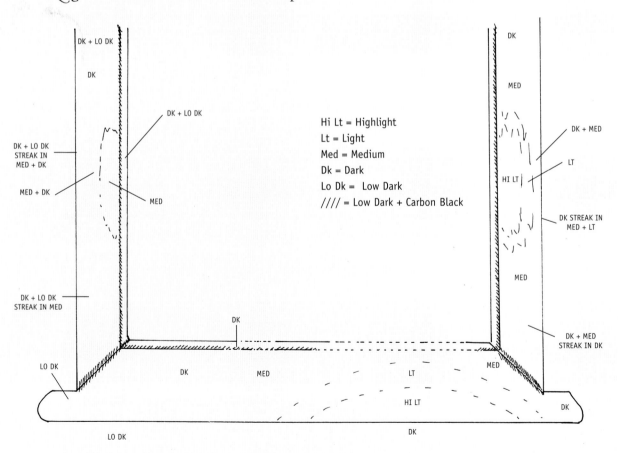

Hi Lt = Highlight
Lt = Light
Med = Medium
Dk = Dark
Lo Dk = Low Dark
//// = Low Dark + Carbon Black

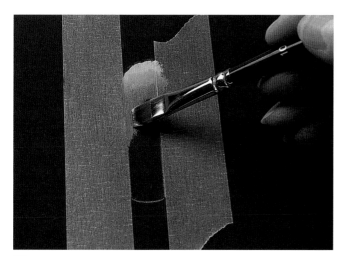

8 Candle

First tape off the candle, then paint it in values. This may take several coats because of the dark blue background.

Candle

Raw Sienna, Cadmium Yellow Mid, Permanent Alizarine, Titanium White, Burnt Umber, Carbon Black

- Medium: RS + CYM + PA
- Light: RS + CYM + TW + medium mix
- Highlight: TW + CYM + RS + tad light mix
- High Dark: Medium mix + RS + PA
- Dark: High dark mix + BU + PA + tad CB
- Low Dark: Dark mix + CB + PA

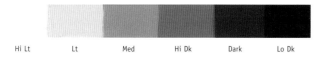

| Hi Lt | Lt | Med | Hi Dk | Dark | Lo Dk |

Candle and Candleholder Value Placement Map

Hi Lt = Highlight
Lt = Light
M or Med = Medium
Dk = Dark
Lo Dk = Low Dark

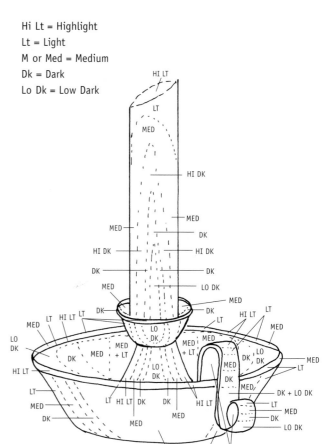

Candle Snuffer Value Placement Map

Hi Lt = Highlight
Lt = Light
M or Med = Medium
Dk = Dark
Lo Dk = Low Dark

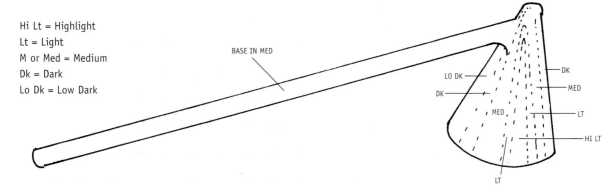

9 Let the values dry, remove the tape, then sand down any hard edges of paint. Paint the drips of wax with the ⅛-inch (3mm) angular brush, using the high dark value down near the bottom and the medium value closer to the top. Then highlight each drip with the light value near the bottom and the highlight value near the top.

10 Matchsticks

Basecoat the top of the sticks using a mixture of the light + dark candle mixes. Base the sides of the sticks with a mix of the dark + low dark candle mixes. Base in the heads with Carbon Black. Highlight the heads using the highlight candleholder mix.

Matchsticks

11 Flame

To enable the flame to be semitransparent and also for the colors to show up on such a dark background, a veil of white is placed on the surface before any more colors are added. Moisten the surface with Retarder and Antiquing Medium. Place a semitransparent application of Titanium White in the area of the flame.

12 Lightly soften the flame with a ¼-inch (6mm) Wee Mop. Allow this wash or veil of color to dry.

13 Remove any graphite lines with odorless solvent and wipe off any excess residue with a clean shop towel. Allow to dry, then seal the entire surface with Clear Glazing Medium. Allow this to dry, then transfer the pattern for the the reflection to the surface.

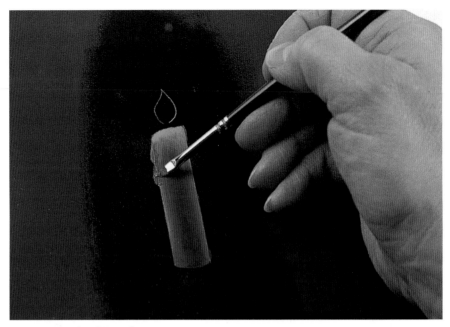

Step 9 Paint the drips of wax.

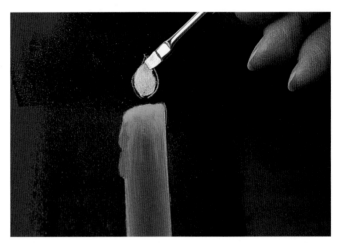

Step 11 Basecoat the flame with semitransparent Titanium White.

Step 12 Soften the flame with a mop brush.

Step 13 Here the value blending and refining is complete.

Reflections

In order for a reflection to be present, you need to have a shiny or reflective surface. In this case, the viewer assumes that glass exists between the window frame and the outside landscape. This reflection must be drawn in the proper perspective with the rest of the design in order for it to be believable. Reflections are mirror images of the objects they reflect, so the viewer will actually see the back sides of the candle and holder. Reflections will have a darker tone than the actual objects themselves and, being transparent, will allow some of the background to show through. To darken the tones, all of the values are moved down a step. So instead of the highlight being the lightest value, the light value will replace the highlight value used in the reflection and Carbon Black will replace the low dark value. Use Retarder and Antiquing Medium to keep the values transparent and blendable. Refer to the value map for the placement of all the values.

Reflection Value Placement Map

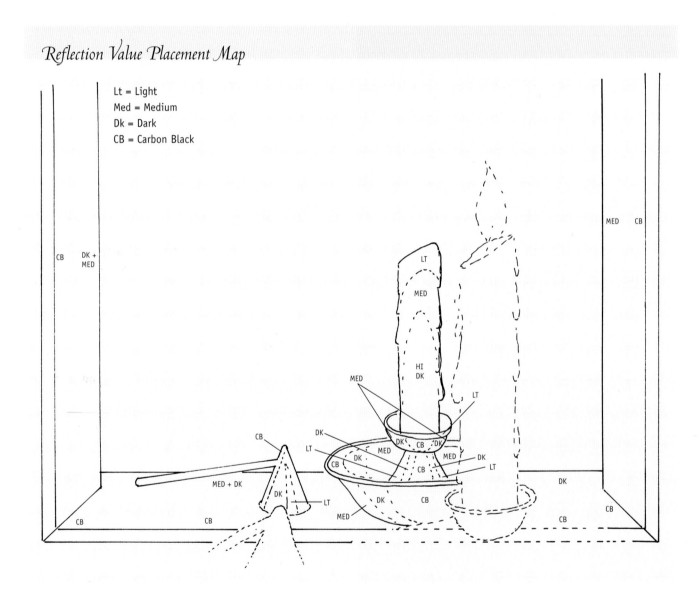

Lt = Light
Med = Medium
Dk = Dark
CB = Carbon Black

14 Reflection Application

Moisten the surface with Retarder and Antiquing Medium. Painting only one object at a time, lightly basecoat the values. Keep the values semitransparent and use a mop brush to soften and blend the values together. This might take several applications of letting the surface dry and reapplying retarder and paint. Clean up any bleeding along the outer edges with a clean brush moistened with water. Once the basic shape of the reflected object is present, remove any graphite lines with odorless solvent and do any touch-up needed.

15 Flame

Moisten the surface of the actual flame with Retarder and Antiquing Medium and apply the colors over the veil of white, referring to the value placement map. Soften with a mop. Paint the reflection of the flame in the same manner as the actual flame, only not as bright.

Flame
- O: Napthol Red Lt + Cadmium Yellow Mid
- RS: Raw Sienna
- WW: Titanium White + Cadmium Yellow Mid
- B: Ultra Blue Deep
- NR: Napthol Red Lt

Flame Value Placement Map

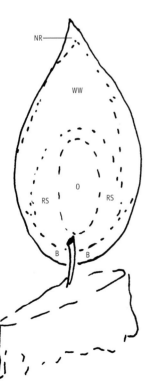

O = Napthol Red Lt + Cadmium Yellow Mid (Orange)
RS = Raw Sienna
WW = Titanium White + tech Cadmium Yellow Mid (Warm White)
B = Ultra Blue Deep
NR = Napthol Red Lt

Highlights, Shading and Shadows

Refer to the glazing map on page 121 for placement. Apply all highlights, shines, shading, glazes and cast shadows to a surface that is moistened with Retarder and Antiquing Medium. Any time you use retarder, use appropriate-sized mops to soften the paint.

16 Sealing

Once the reflections are finished, dry the surface and seal it with one coat of Clear Glazing Medium. Let dry.

17 Window Ledge and Frame

Highlight
1. Using the highlight window ledge mix, strengthen the highlights of the window ledge.
2. Strengthen again using the highlight window ledge mix + Cadmium Yellow Mid + tech Titanium White.

Shading
1. Strengthen the shading using the low dark window ledge mix.
2. Strengthen again, especially the separation areas, using the low dark window ledge mix + Carbon Black.

18 Candleholder and Snuffer

Highlight
1. Strengthen the highlights using the highlight candleholder mix.
2. Strengthen again using the highlight candleholder mix + tad Titanium White + tech Raw Sienna.

Shading
1. Low dark candleholder mix + Carbon Black
2. Carbon Black

19 Candle

Highlight
1. Strengthen the highlights, especially at the top near the flame, using the highlight candle mix.
2. Highlight again using the highlight candle mix + Titanium White + Cadmium Yellow Mid.

Shading
1. Reinforce the shading using the low dark candle mix.

Add a transparent wash of Carbon Black on the reflection next to where it connects to the actual window ledge and frame.

It is not necessary for the reflections to have as many values as the actual objects, so use only three values.

Place a warm glaze of Raw Sienna inside the cup portion of the candleholder as a reflection of the warm glow of the candle flame.

20 Matches

Highlight

1. Highlight using the highlight candle mix.

Shading

1. Shade the top of the matches using the dark candle mix, and the sides of the matches using the low dark candle mix.

21 Flame

Strengthen all of the colors as needed. Place a glow around the flame using a mix of Cadmium Yellow Mid + Napthol Red Lt to create an orange. Please note that this glow is not reflected into the window, so place the glow only around the actual flame.

22 Wick

Base in the wick with Carbon Black, then highlight with the light candleholder mix. Add a spark to the tip of the actual wick with Napthol Red Lt.

23 Reflections

Highlights

1. Strengthen any light and highlight areas as needed. Remember that the reflections will not be as bright as the actual objects.

Shading

1. Using Carbon Black, shade the reflection of the window ledge and frame next to where it connects to the actual frame and at the corner joints.

24 Glazes

Candlelight gives off a warm glow, so to help create this effect, apply a glaze of Cadmium Yellow Mid + tech Titanium White to the light and highlight areas of the window ledge and frame. Glaze Raw Sienna on the inside of the candleholder.

Glazing Map

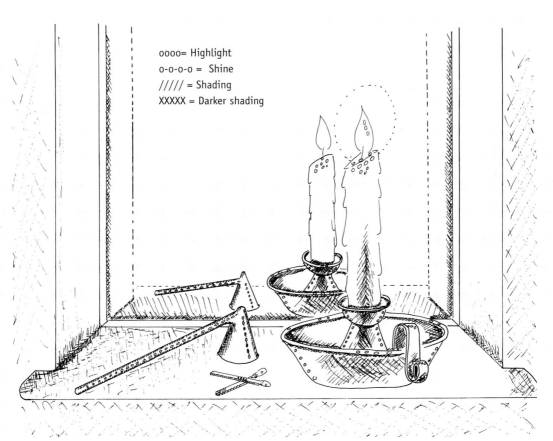

oooo= Highlight
o-o-o-o = Shine
///// = Shading
XXXXX = Darker shading

Add a warm glaze on the window frames across from the flame.

Highlight and shade a few drips in the front of the candle.

Add a glow around the flame. This glow is not seen on the reflection.

Add Warm White for a final shine on the flame.

Bring some of the shadow up onto the actual object to join them together.

Keep this portion of the cast shadow semitransparent to show the distance between the match head and the surface of the ledge.

Paint the cast shadows opaque and very black at the contact points and very transparent at the outer edges.

Add a warm glaze on the window frames across from the flame and on the front of the ledge.

25 Cast Shadows

Paint the cast shadows using Carbon Black and apply them from opaque to semitransparent and then transparent. Because the light source is directly overhead, the cast shadow from the candleholder creates a circular shadow that encompasses the entire bottom of the candleholder. Paint this shadow opaque at the contact point, then let it fade to transparent at the outer edges. The cast shadows from the matchsticks are created from the overhead light of the candle flame. There is some distance from the head of the top match and the window ledge, so paint the shadow under the top match semitransparent where it projects its image onto the window ledge, and make it opaque at the contact points. Paint the cast shadow from the candle snuffer the same as a cast shadow from an upper right-hand light source. It is opaque at the contact point and fades to semitransparent. Remember, you will also see cast shadows in the reflection.

26 Finishing

Seal the surface and frame with a coat of Clear Glazing Medium. Allow this to dry. Antique the frame using a mixture of Brown Earth and Burnt Umber. Dry and apply another coat of Clear Glazing Medium. Dry again and apply at least six coats of varnish.

Color Families

The following are Jo Sonja's Chroma Acrylics categorized into color families, temperatures, values and intensities. Please realize that this is how I categorize them, so it is just one artist's opinion.

The toners (see page 16) and earth colors (see page 15) are noted for each color family. The temperatures are identified as either *W* (warm) or *C* (cool). Some are both warm and cool. Intensities are ranked on a scale from 1 (intense or pure) to 9 (neutralized or very toned). Jo Sonja's Background Colors are also placed into color families, but note that since they are background colors, they are all neutralized and less intense.

	TEMPERATURE	VALUE	INTENSITY
YELLOW			
Warm White	W	Highlight	2
Naples Yellow Hue (earth color)	W	Highlight	7
Cadmium Yellow Light	C	Highlight	1
Yellow Light	W/C	Highlight	1
Cadmium Yellow Mid	W	Light	1
Yellow Deep	W	Light	2
Turners Yellow	W	Light	2
Yellow Oxide (earth color)	W	Low Light	4
Provincial Beige (toner)	W	High Dark	4
Background Color			
Primrose			
Soft White			
YELLOW ORANGE			
Unbleached Titanium	W	White/Highlight	1
Skin Tone Base (toner)	W	Light	6
Indian Yellow	W	Light	1
Fawn (toner)	W	Low Light	4
Raw Sienna (earth color)	W	High Dark	2
ORANGE			
Jaune Brillant	W	Light	1
Cadmium Orange	W	Low Light	1
Norwegian Orange	W	High Dark	4
Gold Oxide (earth color)	W	Dark	7
Background Color			
Cashmere			
Rosehip			
RED ORANGE			
Vermilion	W	Medium	2
Rose Pink (toner)	W	Medium	3
Burnt Sienna (earth color)	W	Dark	2
Brown Madder (earth color)	W	Dark	3
Brown Earth (earth color)	W	Low Dark	1
Background Color			
Blossom			

		TEMPERATURE	VALUE	INTENSITY

RED

	TEMPERATURE	VALUE	INTENSITY
Napthol Red Light	W	Medium	1
Cadmium Scarlet	W	Medium	1
Napthol Crimson	C	Medium	2
Red Earth (earth color)	W	High Dark	6

Background Color

Spice			

RED VIOLET

	TEMPERATURE	VALUE	INTENSITY
Opal (toner)	W	Highlight	6
Amethyst	C	Medium	2
Brilliant Magenta	C	High Dark	4
Plum Pink (toner)	C	High Dark	5
Transparent Magenta	C	Dark	2
Permanent Alizarine	C	Dark	4
Red Violet	C	Dark	2
Burgundy (toner)	C	Dark	4
Purple Madder (earth color)	C	Low Dark	2
Indian Red Oxide (earth color)	W	Low Dark	6

Background Color

Damask Rose			
Deep Plum			

VIOLET

	TEMPERATURE	VALUE	INTENSITY
Brilliant Violet	W	Dark	3
Dioxazine Purple	W	Low Dark	1
Burnt Umber (earth color)	W	Low Dark	6

Background Color

Lavender			

BLUE VIOLET

	TEMPERATURE	VALUE	INTENSITY
Pacific Blue	W	Dark	3
French Blue (toner)	W	Dark	7

Background Color

Azure			

BLUE

	TEMPERATURE	VALUE	INTENSITY
Sapphire (toner)	W	High Dark	5
Cobalt Blue Hue	W	High Dark	1
Ultramarine	W	High Dark	1
Ultra Blue Deep	W	High Dark	1
Pthalo Blue	W/C	Dark	2
Prussian Blue (toner)	C	Low Dark	2
Paynes Grey	W/C	Low Dark/Black	2

Background Color

Sky Blue			
Dolphin Blue			

	TEMPERATURE	VALUE	INTENSITY
BLUE-GREEN			
Colony Blue (toner)	C	Low Light	3
Aqua	C	Low Light	1
Celadon	C	Low Light	3
Antique Green (toner)	W	High Dark	7
Pthalo Green	W/C	Low Dark	1
Teal Green (toner)	C	Low Dark	7
Storm Blue	C	Low Dark/Black	9
Background Color			
Light Teal			
Galaxy Blue			
GREEN			
Nimbus Grey (toner)	W	Light	3
Green Light	W	Medium	2
Jade (toner)	C	Medium	6
Brilliant Green	W	High Dark	2
Green Oxide (earth color)	C	High Dark	6
Hookers Green (toner)	C	Low Dark	5
Background Color			
Dove Grey			
Oakmoss			
Forest Green			
YELLOW-GREEN			
Smoked Pearl (toner)	W	Highlight	4
Moss Green (toner)	W	Highlight	6
Sap Green	W	High Dark	2
Pine Green (toner)	W	Low Dark	3
Olive Green (earth color)	W	Low Dark	9
Raw Umber (earth color)	W	Low Dark	6
Background Color			
Vellum			
Olive Green			

Resources

Paints and Mediums

Jo Sonja's Chroma Acrylics
205 Bucky Dr.
Lititz, PA 17543
www.josonja.com

Brushes

Silver Brush Limited
92 N. Main St., #18E
P.O. Box 414
Windsor, NJ 08561-0414
www.silverbrush.com

Patti DeRenzo
P.O. Box 3385
Crestline, CA 92325
(909) 338-2215
e-mail: pattiderenzo@yahoo.com

Surfaces

Creations in Canvas by Dalee
Available from Viking Woodcrafts, Inc.
1317 Eight St. S.E.
Waseca, MN 56093
(507) 835-3895
Canvas stationery box for the Love Letters project

Custom Wood by Dallas
(Dallas Fisher)
2204 Martha Hulbert Dr.
Lapeere, MI 48446-8091
(800) 251-7154
Cabinet for the Victorian Rose Teacup project

Smooth Cut Wood (Ted Zogg)
P.O. Box 507
Aurora, OR 97002
(503) 678-1318
(888) 982-9663
Cabinet for the New Life project

Valhalla Designs (Jim Rosa)
343 Twin Pines Dr.
Glendale, OR 97442
(541) 832-2732
Tea box for the Tea with Edith project; message board for The Collection Shelf project; calendar for the Let Your Light Shine project

Retailers in Canada

Crafts Canada
2745 29th St. N.E.
Calgary, Alberta T1Y 7B5

Folk Art Enterprises
P.O. Box 1088
Ridgetown, Ontario N0P 2C0
(888) 214-0062

MacPherson Craft Wholesale
83 Queen St. E.
P.O. Box 1870
St. Mary's, Ontario N4X 1C2
(519) 284-1741

Maureen McNaughton Enterprises
Rt. 2
Bellwood, Ontario N0B 1J0
(519) 843-5648

Mercury Art and Craft Supershop
332 Wellington St.
London, Ontario N6C 4P7
(519) 434-1636

Town and Country Folk Art Supplies
93 Green Ln.
Thornhill, Ontario L3T 6K6
(905) 882-0199

Retailers in the United Kingdom

Art Express
Index House
70 Burley Road
Leeds LS3 1JX
0800 731 4185
www.artexpress.co.uk

Atlantis Art Materials
146 Brick Lane
London E1 6RU
020 7377 8855

Crafts World (head office)
No 8 North Street, Guildford
Surrey GU1 4AF
07000 757070

Hobby Crafts (head office)
River Court
Southern Sector
Bournemouth International Airport
Christchurch
Dorset BH23 6SE
0800 272387

Homecrafts Direct
PO Box 38
Leicester LE1 9BU
0116 251 3139

Index